MULTIPLE CHURCH STAFF HANDBOOK

MULTIPLE CHURCH STAFF HANDBOOK

Harold J. Westing

Foreword by Donald L. Bubna

KREGEL PUBLICATIONS
Grand Rapids, Michigan 49501

We acknowledge with appreciation the permission to reprint the following copyrighted material:

Artwork for chapter 2, copyright 1979; for chapter 3, copyright 1981; chapter 5, copyright 1979; and for chapter 6, copyright 1982: all by Larry Thomas. Artwork for chapter 4, copyright 1981 by Erik D. Johnson. Artwork for chapter 10, Larry Thomas, copyright 1981; chapter 11, Mary Chambers, copyright 1981 and for chapter 13, Larry Thomas, copyright 1982: all by *Leadership Journal*. All used by permission and special arrangements.

Library of Congress Cataloging in Publication Data

Westing, Harold J., 1929-
Multiple Church-staff Handbook.

Bibliography: p.
Includes index.
1. Church officers—Handbooks, manuals, etc.
2. Church management—Handbooks, manuals, etc.
3. Christian leadership—Handbooks, manuals, etc.
I. Title.
BV705.W46 1985 254 85-9811
ISBN 0-8254-4031-9

Printed in the United States of America

DEDICATION

THIS BOOK IS dedicated with deep appreciation to my son and son-in-law. Currently Tom Westing serves as an associate minister of a church in New Mexico, where he is learning the honor of being on a harmonious church staff. Bruce Martin, who is in Italy with the Conservative Baptist Foreign Mission Society, is living out a lifelong dream of planting a church with a team in a cross-cultural context.

CONTENTS

Foreword by Donald L. Bubna 9
Introduction 11

PART I: Concerning the Team

Chapter 1. Teamwork Is the Goal of the Church 14
Project 23

Chapter 2. Every Team Needs a Leader 24
The lead pastor plays the key role in the selection of the staff 30; becomes a staff enabler 31; as coordinator for responsibilities 32; as truster and supporter 34; as communicator 35; as pastor to the staff 36; *Project* 37

Chapter 3. Teams Must Face Their Problems 40
Singleness is better 41; Potential team problems 44; *Project* 57

PART II: The Functioning of a Team

Chapter 4. Maintaining a Balanced Team 58
Adding team members 63; Keeping the balance 64; *Project* 67

Chapter 5. What Makes the Glue? 72
The family's feelings of roots 74; The corporate drive for productivity 76; The athlete's commonly owned goal 78; The theologian's binding issues 79; The marriage's common commitment 80; The scientist's studied insight 81; *Project* 83

Chapter 6. Describing Your Mission 86
Advantages of job descriptions 88; Job description ingredients 90; Overcoming dangers of job descriptions 91; *Project* 94; Job description for staff members 95

Chapter 7. Clarifying Your Role Expectations 100
The role clarification process 102; Facing the risks 103; The facilitator's role 104; Negotiating role expectations 105

Chapter 8. Managing Upward 108
Misconceptions about managing upward 109; Need for managing upward 110; Procedure for managing upward 112

PART III: Maintaining the Team
Chapter 9. The Staff Meeting 118
Staff philosophy 120; Staff meeting agenda 125; *Project* 134
Chapter 10. The Staff Retreat 136
The setting 138; The working agenda 140; *Project* 143
Chapter 11. Hiring New Staff 144
When not to add new staff 145; When to add new staff 149; Preparing the church 151; The search committee 155; Searching for candidates 157; *Project* 159
Chapter 12. Conducting the Interview 162
Guidelines for the search committee 164; Qualities to look for 166; Pastoral style of leadership 171; Guidelines for candidating 175; *Project* 178
Chapter 13. Financial Equity of the Team 180
Determining equity 184; *Project* 186; Special considerations 192; Personal finances 193

APPENDIX: Philosophy of Ministry 197
Notes 205
Bibliography 207

DIAGRAMS:
Philosophy Statement 18
Christian and Worldly Leadership Model Contrasted 27
Role and Title Chart 45
Johari Window 52
Four Styles of Leadership 61
Biblical Leadership 63
True Team Approach 66
Temperament Test 69
Your Management Temperament Profile 70
Temperaments 71
Church Committees 98
Board/staff Relationship 99
Sunday Staff Assignments 131
Work Calendar 142
Pastor's Priorities 159
Pastoral Style of Leadership 172

FOREWORD

STAFF RELATIONS can lead to triumph and tragedy.

Some of my best friends are fellow staff members. Their presence, support and stimulation bring me great joy. They also often make me look good. I love being with them. I love to see them succeed. My team is made up of some of my favorite people.

My deepest wounds in ministry have also come from people on my staff. Those closest to us can hurt us most. To be vulnerable with colleagues, sets us up to be hurt. It is part of the risk in leadership. This experience is echoed by hundreds of pastors across North America.

Harold J. Westing has been in the trenches as a staff member. He knows the joy and pain of ministry together. He writes as a practitioner and teacher. He has consulted with hundreds of church staff including my own.

He writes from a solid biblical and psychological base that gives credibility to his wide use of illustrations and practical helps. President Hadden Robinson calls him "one of the best communicators on our faculty at Denver Seminary."

I have worked with Harold Westing in pastor's conferences for almost twenty years. He has deeply touched my life as a colleague, consultant and stimulating friend.

He has a deep commitment to the local church. Here is excellent help for developing a multiple staff. Readers will get handles on goal setting, role clarification, conducting staff meetings and leadership retreats. Each chapter recommends work projects for application with your team. Seminary professors will find this book ideal for classroom use.

A great number of churches are moving toward a multiple staff, even smaller churches. Often this begins with volunteers, interns or part-time professional people who meet weekly with the senior pastor. The specialization of youth, Christian Education and music ministries necessitate this. No longer can one person, even in a small church, be expected to give leadership to so many important areas. Pastors will find this volume very helpful in getting started right with their team.

Here's for more triumphs and fewer tragedies for the multiple staff.

DONALD L. BUBNA

Senior Pastor
Salem Alliance Church
Salem, Oregon
Contributing editor to *Leadership Journal*

INTRODUCTION

IT IS NOT biblical to think of ministering alone. The New Testament is the history of men and women working side by side in ministry. For centuries the laity have shown us some models of true teamwork. We have seen them in youth ministries, city missions, church educational programs, foreign missions, evangelistic projects and similar activities. On the other hand, for decades a large majority of the clergy have worked alone, often in isolation, and thus too often in frustration.

With the recent growth of the evangelical churches, the emphasis on spiritual gifts, and the finances to pay for additional staff, the clergy have been brought together to work as teams. But current history has not given us many good models. My thirty-five years of involvement with hundreds of church multiple-staffs is most depressing. It is rare to find one out of four multiple staffs working in love and harmony. Many team members merely tolerate each other. They resemble married couples living together like singles who have no commitment, common goals or sense of sharing. They simply share the same house.

If there is any place in the Christian world where people ought to be a genuine team, it is in the leadership of the church. The pastoral staff should be a model of all that Christ intended the church to be. To please the Father is to work in unity. Church leadership should demonstrate the genuine working out of diversity of gifts. The pastoral staff should show how acceptance, forgiveness, sharing, supporting, encouraging and the accomplishment of common goals is practiced. The staff must be a microcosm of the body of Christ, a church in miniature. If the pastoral staff can't demonstrate to God's people the beauty and harmony of the body of Christ, its members can't expect the church family to function together adequately.

This book is written out of a great concern that church staff teams be godly microcosms, so that church members will see models of how they ought to work side by side.

As you read this book, you may feel I'm being too idealistic at times. I have seen or participated in everything of which I speak in these chapters. In all my years of ministry, privileged to be a member of a team, I have experienced the prosperity of genuine godly teamwork, as well as the agony of so-called teams who could hardly tolerate each other. Struggling with my own selfish humanity, I have learned the joy and fulfillment of a pilgrimage with other men and women who were seeking to work out a harmonious godly microcosm.

These lessons have been hammered out during the years I have been a member of five church-staff teams, a member of a state and national church association team, and finally as a member of the faculty of a seminary. During the last twenty years, as a consultant to churches where the scenarios in this book were lived out, I have cried or rejoiced with hundreds of others who struggled with these same issues in trying to be a godly microcosm. Also, during that period of time, I was heavily involved in placing staff members on church teams.

My prayer is that you will come to know an enriched ministry through the outworking of the principles in these chapters.

This book is designed to give you motivation and guidelines for developing a godly team. For that to happen, every member of your team should read and discuss the chapters together. Make it a part of the agenda of each week's staff meeting. The projects at the end of the chapters will provide the framework to facilitate those discussions. Ample projects are included to help you explore and aid the development of your team on staff retreats, which is a must for a growing church staff.

MULTIPLE CHURCH-STAFF HANDBOOK

Part I: **Concerning the Team**

1

TEAMWORK IS THE GOAL OF THE CHURCH

"Don't you think this is carrying the *team*-spirit a bit too far?"

1

TEAMWORK IS THE GOAL OF THE CHURCH

SEVENTY-FIVE THOUSAND fans are crammed into the mile-high stadium in Denver. They have come to see their favorite Denver Broncos play football. They didn't come to watch the huddle or the lineup at the scrimmage. They stamp their feet and cheer at the top of their lungs when the offensive line holds off the defensive line. Meanwhile, the tight-end breaks into the open and makes a breathtaking catch in the end zone, with a winning touchdown in the remaining moments of the game. Every player who is interviewed by the announcer at the end of the game praises the other players, who all played unselfishly so the team could display their powerful potential by becoming champs. That team, like any other team, is successful in proportion to the way each team member works in harmony with the rest.

As Paul is showing the church at Ephesus their great potential for being a growing, producing, and loving church, he says, "We are to grow up in . . . Him . . . from whom the whole body, being fitted and held together by that which every joint supplies, according to the proper working of each individual part, causes the growth of the body for the building up of itself in love" (Eph. 4:15-16).

The two most essential elements in the success of the church, Paul says, are to make sure that each member does the thing for which he is best equipped, and to make sure that those joints (fellowship connections) keep working properly. Christ will flow from one member to another through the connecting fellowship and communication joints. If you hamper either of those, you have shut down the team and its productivity. Paul had just finished saying that the church team could display the glory of God and His mighty power in a way the members had not yet comprehended or even dared to dream of (Eph. 3:20-21). We can do that in every generation if we will work as a team should work (Eph. 4). God has planned that we should have unlimited creative power in this world if we will only learn to work together in His designed way.

If God is expecting the church to function as a team, it's only logical that the church staff must model how a team is to function. That's the thesis of this book. How can we expect the Church of Jesus Christ to function as a team if the church staff doesn't model teamwork? A team is a group of God's people which utilizes to the ultimate the gifts God has given them and which works in beautiful fellowship connection within itself.

God said the same thing to Israel in Genesis 11:6: "Nothing which they purpose to do will be impossible for them." There were two reasons why this mighty team of people could have such potential. Genesis 11:6 says that they were *one* people. They were an edified body with one common goal. Evidence showed good communication by the use of a common language. God said, "Let them own a common goal and see that they keep open communication channels, and you can't keep them from succeeding at any task."

The problem was that their common goal — to build a tower to reach the heavens and make themselves a mighty name — was contrary to God's purpose. So He confused their language. He stopped the flow of their communication.

Visiting a church in California recently, we saw a model of a team-style church. The members worked hand-in-hand to help each one function with a small group of people in some ministry during the week, such as an evangelistic home Bible study, discipleship group, or outreach ministry. Their newly acquired computer kept records of where all their people were ministering. Of the 3500 people who attended church on Sunday, slightly over 3000 were involved that week in some team effort.

After I learned this, I could better understand the high level of excitement around the church facilities on Sunday morning. Everyone seemed to know someone else who cared for him or her. They were excited because they were part of a special work of God.

One couldn't help but contrast that situation with another large church I had attended earlier. We would classify this second group as a spectator church. The people came for the entertainment. It was good that they attended and were being fed the Word of God. But they, by virtue of the role they were playing, were being trained to be passive rather than learning to be active participants in building the body of Christ.

I was soon to learn the secret of the model team church. Their paid staff was a true microcosm of the way the whole church was to function. Each member was accountable to other team members for the utilization of his gifts. There was great communication among the teams at the weekly departmental and general staff meetings.

Pages of church history record the stories of God's people doing great exploits for Him — healing, saving, and restoring broken communities. Often these movements were brought to a halt, not because they had the wrong objectives, but because they lost sight of their common cause or because they allowed their communication lines to be broken.

The pastor and his staff must be pace-setters in the process of building a sense of common purpose in the congregation. That can be done in numerous ways, but the more people who participate in the process, the more the congregation can own it, and the more unity there will be in its fulfillment.

Entering the narthex of a church in Oregon on a Sunday morning, I was struck by the unusual. Every wall in the large hall was hung with newsprint covered with handwritten notes from Friday and Saturday's all-workers yearly planning session. The discussions reflected on those sheets became a major factor in turning the church around from a spiral of decline.

Since the staff ought to be part of the leadership team which carries out the common purpose of the church, the staff should play a major role in forming the church's philosophy.

Every church's philosophy statement should reflect the uniqueness of that particular congregation. God has spent much effort in making us all unique. Since each congregation is a composite personality, and thus a unique one, we shouldn't try to make all churches alike. On a map draw a five-mile radius around your church location. Determine what is unique about your church compared to all those other congregations in that circle.

In America today numerous churches exist in just about every city and neighborhood. Each community represents a diverse group of people with various personalities, backgrounds, and needs. Peter Wagner in his book, *Our Kind of People,* suggests that America is not a melting pot, but a group of homogeneous peoples. Consequently, it is only wise that we do not try to duplicate each other.

Some churches, because of their location and the group of people who attend the services, ought to concentrate on senior citizens, while others on college/career-age people. Some churches will provide a strong teaching ministry, while others will have a far more effective evangelistic thrust. Because of that diversity each congregation needs a different philosophy.

Before a church staff and congregation can determine the strategy for its ministry, it must know its own philosophy of ministry. Its philosophy statement must be built on God's Word and will be a reflection of the interpretation of how this unique congregation works out those biblical tenets.

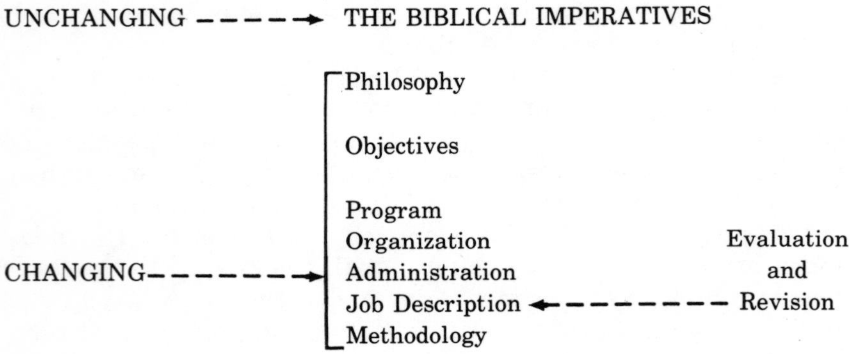

A good philosophy statement will include some, if not all, of the following items:

Priorities of evangelism and discipleship
What you understand discipleship to mean
The use of spiritual gifts in the body
The role of the staff
The emphasis you give the building
The place and methods of Bible teaching
The style of government
Guidelines of accountability
What you see as the major goal of the body
Relationships within the body
Decision-making process and authority
The order of your priorities
Recruitment of the leadership team
The importance of the facility
The place of worship and music
A statement about ultimate size

It's wise to have this philosophy statement (see Appendix for a model) basically worked out in the early stages of the church's development. The church without such a statement will be like a ship trying to find its way in the harbor without a rudder. It may drift around without a destination and never find its proper port.

This book gives a prominent place to church philosophy on church staff, because the way a staff functions is determined by its church's philosophy statement.

For the congregation wishing to develop a philosophy statement, the following procedural guidelines are suggested.

1. Give the congregation a clear-cut rationale for developing a philosophy. Encourage the members to begin thinking about what concepts should eventually be included in their philosophy statement.
2. In order to form a biblical foundation for its philosophy, a congregation should study the mission of the church. The pastor should preach a series of sermons from such books as Acts, Ephesians, and Corinthians. Adult Bible study classes should be guided in similar studies.

   Present all options for styles and emphasis of ministries. Provide a reading list of books on the subjects of church planting, development, and growth. Circulate key magazine articles among the congregation.
3. Hold one or two open hearings for the congregation so the members can discuss the major concepts they would like to see included. Emphasize that this is a preliminary discussion and all decisions will be finalized later. These meetings will provide opportunity for members to ask questions and learn what others are thinking.
4. Set aside a block of time, preferably a retreat, and bathe the whole event in prayer. The entire congregation should be urged to attend. Divide the group into work/study teams of thirteen to seventeen people of various ages. Each team should write, in outline form, some concepts to be part of the church's philosophy statement. It is of utmost importance to assign priorities to the various items.

   First Baptist Church of Modesto, California, has taken great care to state its priorities in this order: a) evangelism; b) discipleship; c) staff; and d) facilities. That is a major part of the church's philosophy statement. No decision about any expenditure of time or finances, or of program development is made without giving serious consideration to the order of these priorities. For instance, the church puts more money into staff than into extravagant buildings. This doesn't mean they don't build buildings; but when they built their 2000-plus-seat auditorium, it was a stand-up, reinforced concrete warehouse-type building with an attractive mansard-style roof. It was built for about half the price of a normal church edifice. The funds that might have gone into the auditorium instead went into more staff, because that was higher on their priority list.

More and more churches are changing their priorities about where their congregational energies are expended. The saints need to be released from maintenance work and placed into outreach type ministries. A study of Frank Tillapaugh's book, *The Church Unleashed,* would give you further illustrations on priorities.

5. Assign someone with writing and analytical skills to take all of the reports and make a composite which will include all the statements. Of course there will be repetition of many ideas stated in numerous ways. The editor's task will be to make sure that each unique idea is included and is stated in the most meaningful way. The editor should prepare an orderly first draft which will go back to the congregation for its ratification.
6. A final congregational meeting will be called to discuss the composite work. At that time, no doubt, there will be some word changes, and discussions about why certain points or statements ought or ought not to be included. All of the congregation who participate will gain a marvelous education about the meaning of the local body of Christ, as well as come to own their church's mission.

You may question the amount of time and energy needed to complete this process. The pastor, his staff, or the church boards could much more readily draw up a document that would be equally well written. But keep in mind your objective. It is not how quickly it's written that counts, but who owns it. People will work towards the accomplishment of their church's mission in proportion to the clarity and ownership of its goals.

No doubt you will continue to rework the original version as the years go by, but each decision made by the congregation and staff will only tend to endear the church to their hearts and strengthen the team's ministry. The philosophy statement should constantly be referred to in preaching, training sessions, business meetings, and even when announcements are made.

It should be referred to in all church documents, including any promotional pieces about the church.

So God has said in His Word that teams who have a clearly agreed upon objective, and who keep their communication lines open, can do great exploits for God. A strong church staff will always keep these major factors before them. It is important to note the fact that the Holy Spirit gives multiple and diverse gifts, so that each member of the body can play a special part in the construction of Christ's church (1 Cor. 12 and Romans 12).

Note also that Ephesians 4:10-12 states that Christ gave gifts to the church. Those four gifts embodied in persons are often referred to as the ascension gifts, since Christ gave them to the church as He ascended on high. It is logical to conclude, therefore, that Christ expected it would take a team of people to build the church.

The Bible gives numerous other commands and advantages of working together as a team. Some of these will be highlighted here.

Often we conceive of Paul as an individualist until we reflect on all of his partners in ministry. Thirteen different teams are mentioned relating to his life and work, and twenty-two other teams are referred to in the New Testament. No wonder we find some churches which go back to the Scriptures for a fresh study about church structure and decide to have a multiple elder-style rule.

A pastoral staff can better function as a team, for a team has these advantages:

1. *Teams allow for cross training of each other* (1 Cor. 3:7-8 and John 4:37-38). Just as Paul planted and Apollos watered, so each team member can bring his own unique understanding of God's Word to the congregation.

   We are seeing a growing number of congregations with co-preaching pastors who do a beautiful job of doing just that. One is better at evangelizing and the other stronger at nurturing. Some Friends congregations, with their multiple preaching elders, practice this in a wholesome way. In situations such as this, they not only bring a greater breadth and richness to the congregation, but also they better equip each other for ministry.
2. *Team productivity is greatly heightened* (Prov. 11:14; 15:22; 24:6; Eccl. 4:9-13). The wisdom of the writer in these passages helps us understand a new kind of addition. Each individual worker/laborer can produce a certain level of

fruit. The writer suggests that by putting two workers' efforts together, it will more than equal the sum of the two, because each one sharpens the other's mind and heart, making each more productive.

One significant example of this can be found in the broadened outreach a team has over that of one member. The uniqueness of each personality draws certain homogeneous grouping to the church. Dr. W. A. Criswell of the First Baptist Church of Dallas has found that within a year, a new staff person ought to be able to attract at least ten new families, if he is functioning on a normal level of efficiency. Dr. Criswell sees that as a good investment, since in a short time staff people will pay their own way and will greatly enhance the outreach of the church.

3. *Teams encourage and protect each other.* They provide companionship (2 Tim. 4:21), encouragement (Acts 28:15), and burden sharing (Hebrews 10:33).

   No doubt many a former Christian worker would not have left his or her post of service had there been someone with whom to share the burdens. It takes an unusually stable soul to do battle alone "against the world, the flesh and the devil."

4. *Teams build a ministry more quickly* because of group incentive (Heb. 10:24), because priorities are kept (Acts 6:2-7), and because they provide leadership for persons who are not naturally leaders (1 Thess. 4:12).

5. *Teams can help keep the church honest* as it makes decisions about the outworking of its theology in its ministry.

   Dody Donnelly suggests in this book, *Team,*[1] that each person perceives each issue through what he calls the "See-Level" (a combination of one C and 4 E's — CE4). A person is the product of his or her **C**ulture, **E**ducation, **E**xperience, **E**nvironment, and **E**xpectation. Donnelly suggests that each person has a different perceptual mechanism. Some people have a tremendous sense of perception to the point that we would call it the gift of wisdom. However, even these people do not see all the issues because of the limitation of their "See-Level."

   Every time you add a new person to the staff, the depth of perception on any given issue will be greatly heightened. Therefore, decisions will be far more honest, or accurate.

Peter Drucker suggests that when a team sits down to make an administrative decision, the members need to be sure they have seen all the possibilities and loopholes. He even goes so far as to suggest that if you can't find any reason for not moving in a certain direction, that you perhaps better not do so. He feels that you haven't found all the issues yet. An open, honest team will greatly aid you in finding all the issues involved. When you act, make sure you do so with a knowledge of all the issues at stake.

Current church growth studies indicate that churches which start with a large group have a much better chance of growing than those which are started with one dedicated individual or couple. Groups attract more people than individuals do. Not only does each individual's personality attract those of like kind, but sociologists have known for a long time that the mixture of those personalities have a unique attractiveness of their own.

Certain home and foreign mission societies have been practicing this team principle for years and have seen the gospel spread rapidly because of their team efforts.

Teamwork is one of the major principles you will need to follow if you wish to pattern yourself after the New Testament church. The Godhead designed the church and equipped it with the essential gifts for teamwork, with a built-in guarantee that God will make you much more productive in His work, when all of you put your hands to the common plow.

Project for Chapter 1

Design a working draft of a church philosophy for your church. Since later you will want your whole congregation to be involved in the process as outlined in this chapter, it is important for you to think through a philosophy you would be comfortable with. This will be helpful in guiding church members in the formation of their own philosophy statement. Check the list in this chapter of items that should be included in a complete church philosophy. For additional suggestions, note the model statement of South Evangelical Presbyterian Fellowship in the Appendix.

Part I: **Concerning the Team**

2

EVERY TEAM NEEDS A LEADER

"From now on we're going to operate as a theocracy . . . and I'm Theo."

2

EVERY TEAM NEEDS A LEADER

WE HAVE ESTABLISHED that God's plan is for the church to function as a team, and for the church staff to function as a microcosm of that body.

Many married people really live together as singles, even though they went through a marriage ceremony. In the same way, too many church staff people could be classified as team singles. They think and plan singly. They aren't concerned about how they affect the rest of the team; consequently, most of what they do is done alone. Christ's high priestly prayer in John 17 was an earnest plea that the body of Christ, which is *one*, would learn to function in unity or oneness. Marvin Judy views the multiple staff as an "organismic" ministry, that is, each person on the staff is an entity in himself; but he is also a part of the total organism. The Romans would call their leader, "primus-iter-pares" — first among equals.

It seems ironic that once having established that the church staff is a team, we need to mention the idea of a leader. Some leaders argue that the model of the New Testament church is multiple elder rule (they interpret that as meaning a multiplicity of bosses) without a leader. Even though teams or multiple elder rule is suggested in the New Testament, it does not of necessity suggest that there is no leader among the team.

A biblical principle, with its roots in the Godhead, in Genesis, and in the creation of man, stresses the team leader concept. As God the Father is head of the Godhead, and husbands are head of the wives, so a leader or pastor/shepherd must be head of a local assembly. Keep in mind, however, another important part of that principle. There is diversity of function among equals. The headship, or role of leader, does not destroy equality. The husband is to be the head, but that doesn't destroy the equality of the husband and wife.

The pastor is to be chief of staff, which is a way of working, not a way of showing power or preference. He becomes a chief among equals. He takes on a burden, not a privilege, as team leader. There are few model senior pastors who understand and practice the "headship equal" principle among their staff. If they pick up their clues from the worldly system of leadership rather than the biblical model of servant/leadership, they find themselves lording it over others, rather than working with them. From the standpoint of the associate, there is no equivocation about who is the leader of the team. The pastor is the leader. He is the pastor of each associate on the pastoral team. A staff in the local church is like a quartet — it needs one good lead. That lead must realize that he needs three other parts to support and harmonize his ministry, so that he does not stand out as the lead. The group together brings harmony and unity to the total leadership of the staff.

The true servant/leader has embedded in his mind the concept of making others look great and successful. No place is that better illustrated than in the short parable of the Grateful Servant in Luke 17. Here the servant is shown as one who works to make his master look good, and he does it without any thought of commendation, consideration, or conceit. After a hard day in the field, the slave comes in and waits upon his master, fulfilling all his needs. The slave's only concern is to make his master look good.

As Howard Butt states in his book, *Velvet Covered Brick*, "He serves by leading and leads by serving." The pastor helps to fulfill the dreams and aspirations of those who work on his team. He serves their best interest, not his own.

Don Bubna, an Oregon pastor, suggests three ways of looking at leadership. The worldly view says, "Leadership is getting things done through people your way." A second view, which is often falsely thought of as a Christian view of leadership, suggests, "A leader gets things done through people." That kind of leader may include others in the process. Thirdly, the genuine servant-style of leadership suggests, "A leader gets people done (mature) through things (events and program)." This third view pinpoints the long-range objectives of any and all events, and the ultimate maturity or completion of people who are aided in their growth toward Christian adulthood. Of course, if they are to grow, they will be involved in the total process of planning and implementing the events which will help them grow. A servant/leader then is more concerned with what is going on in people's lives, than he is in what the program looks like.

The spirit of a shepherd/leader is also exemplified in the model Christ gave, "Whoever wishes to become great among you shall be your servant, and whoever wishes to be first among you shall be your slave; just as the Son of Man did not come to be served, but to serve, and to give His life a ransom for many" (Matt. 20:26-28).

You might understand that better if you contrast it with the worldly corporate leadership model. A major goal in that system is to climb the corporate ladder. In order to do that it takes *others* serving *your* best interest. If you can climb over enough people to fight your way to the top, you can become the president of your company. It takes all those people working on your behalf to get you there and keep you there. They are serving your personal interest in order to fill your need for power.

Too often Christian leadership books depict Christian leaders doing the same. You've seen the pictures.

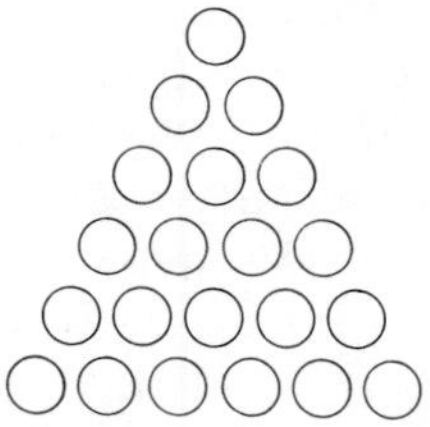

Sometimes the pictures are even on the covers of their books. But wait a minute, doesn't Jesus talk about making others president? No, I believe He goes one step further than that. Every promotion is downward, at least in spirit if not in position. The picture should look like this, with Jesus at the very bottom.

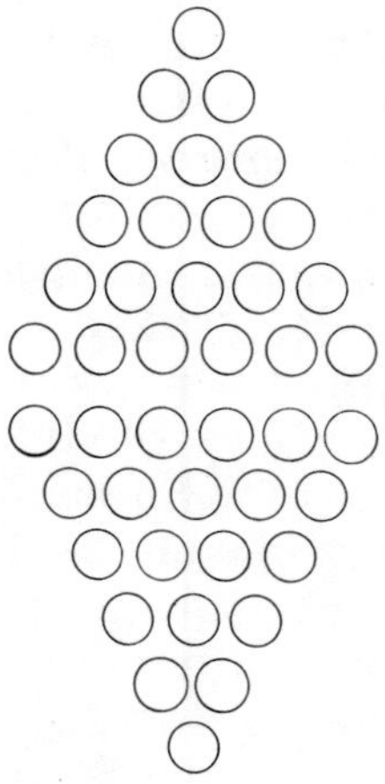

A leader, like Christ, works downward so he can support or develop even more people. He takes the lowly position because he wants to fulfill the others. That's what Christ did in redemption, by giving us peace, and in sanctification, by giving us maturity. He was truly making us great.

The lead pastor will do everything he can to make the youth pastor successful in directing the youth. He wants the Christian education director to have the most capable and gifted people on his team so the Sunday school will flourish. He won't influence all of the strong leadership of the church to join the boards he works with, and leave the less gifted to work with the other staff.

Another strong guideline in the New Testament concerns the function of the team leader. The church gets its theological foundation from the Book of Ephesians, with the staff receiving strong directions from Ephesians 4. Notice the ascension gifts of Christ given to the church so the church will be edified. Paul says that Christ has given pastor-teachers to the church, so they will be equipped. That word *equipped* means that he will *direct their spiritual exercise*. He will see that they are godly, or that they practice their righteousness, and he will see that they do the work of love and righteousness. Here is a major word, not only about the need for a leader, but the leader's role. He will lead the members in their spiritual exercise, and he will lead his staff. That means helping them in their personal relationships to God and guiding them in exercising their spiritual gifts.

Even when there are only two staff members, someone is in charge. He is the key to an effective staff, just as he is to the spiritual life of the body. In fact, if the health of the staff is strong, it ultimately will be reflected in the health of the congregation. The team's health and cooperation will be of utmost importance to him. He will work on it as a married man does his marriage, because he knows that the maturity of his children depends upon the maturity of his marriage.

He is responsible for shaping the operation, cooperation, and ministry of his staff. He can't delegate that to another staff member totally. In a large team, second-level supervision will be necessary because a leader shouldn't have more than six people directly relating to him. So a children's worker might be accountable to the Christian education director, who in turn is accountable to the senior pastor.

A situation in which it is difficult for a pastor to lead a team is illustrated by the following story. Mark served as a Christian education director for eight years with a harmonious and productive team. A door of opportunity opened in another city for him to be senior pastor of a church with three staff members. He expected to duplicate that same teamwork in his new role. Because he had headed up the youth program and directed the total Christian education program, he knew what he wanted in the staff people who would serve under him in those capacities.

But the whole scene was different now. He had a new congregation to deal with, plus a new set of group dynamics coming out of the unique personalities of new team members. It was not what he had expected. In addition, he now had to learn to lead, whereas before he thought as a Number Two man thinks. It was hard for him to see the church programs go in a direction other than what he preferred. Because a pastor can lead in one set of circumstances doesn't guarantee that he can do so in another. Each addition to the staff affects the whole staff. The complexity of the corporate personality changes, and each member of the team must be ready to accept that change.

When things go wrong with the team's relationship, the senior pastor usually gets the blame. Other staff members are often too quick to point the finger at their leader. In most cases, the senior pastor would be expected to take the lead in restoring healthy communication. But if a team has been functioning as a team should, it is possible that another team member might take the initiative in healing the breach. Our experience shows that in a large majority of the cases, the rest of the staff expects their leader to initiate staff meetings, and maintain open relationships and open communications. If a pastor isn't willing to take on that responsibility, perhaps he shouldn't become the senior minister of a large church with a multiple staff.

Another example of a time a leader will find it hard to lead concerns Pastor Roberts, who had a most successful ministry in Iowa in a town of 12,000 people. His congregation of 150 thought so highly of him that they didn't want him to leave. He was a true shepherd-style pastor who genuinely cared for each member. No wonder a large church in Illinois called him to become their pastor. No one had told them that one pastor can care deeply for a maximum of about 185 people. It didn't take many months after arriving at his new charge before he realized how different things were. Now he had to share the limelight with two full-time staff people. He had to learn to work through them. Now he needed to delegate responsibility. Now the administration was different. He had to be concerned with the proper lines of communication. He couldn't make decisions quickly with the

Sunday school superintendent without bypassing the Christian education minister. He thought that by having additional staff to work with, he could really enhance his ministry, but instead it led to frustration.

Many pastors find it easier to work alone. But if the leader sees the benefit of a team, he will realize that by working with others, he can deepen the ministry.

One minister was assisted by Mr. Peters, his only staff member. Mr. Peters, a strong layman, was like the tribal chief to the congregation in that he cared for most of the administrative decisions. He had helped found the church and felt a strong sense of vested interest. He and the pastor got along famously well, since the pastor dealt personally with the people's ills and needs by preaching and counseling, but he was not an administrator.

When the pastor moved to another church, he found himself in the midst of administering a staff. He could not delegate that to someone else. Here the congregation expected him to lead the staff, as well as the congregation. Because he hadn't learned the skills of doing that in the past, it was hard for him to know how to function as an administrator, so he left those details alone, hoping that they would go away. He became like the Israelites wishing again for their former land of Egypt.

When a multiple-staff church calls a new lead pastor, the members need to question their candidate thoroughly about his ability and desires to be an administrator. The pastor, as well, must think carefully before he accepts a call to such a church. Will he be willing to give the time and attention necessary to work with a staff? If not, he may find his relationship with the team other than ideal. It becomes sheer agony and often ends up in "divorce" with staff members who come only for a short stay.

As the chief of staff among equals, the lead pastor has a special role to play. Here we will speak of his task more than the attitude with which he approaches his task.

The Lead Pastor Should Play the Key Role in the Selection of the Staff

It would be folly for the lead pastor to take the full responsibility for choosing additional team members. The senior pastor should serve as the chairperson of the selection committee (if you choose to use the committee approach). He should have a strong say about the final selection, because their personalities and goals must be compatible. The resumes and the initial written and phone references can be gathered by other team members or committee persons. The pastor will want to spend ample time with the candidate to obtain facts and impressions, so he can wisely influence the final selection process.

A person's strengths and how they complement the team will be a major factor to consider when making that final selection. You will probably want to add a specialist rather than a generalist. How will he complement the rest of the team? He should have a strength that other team members don't have both in temperament and ministry skills.

The appropriate church voting board should ratify the selection made by the staff. In case of strong congregational role, the congregation should make the final vote.

A church was going to hire its sixth team member. Pastor Carlson was anxious to hire a long-time friend. The pastor was certain the staff would not deny his wishes. The man was interviewed by the whole team. The pastor was wise in listening to their insight, but unwise in turning down their recommendation not to hire his friend. After the new man came, he was not accepted into the team. He had Pastor Carlson's strong support, but that became a block against the rest of the team, and the team's harmony was soon destroyed. Pastor Carlson was blinded by his friendship and this kept him from seeing the weaknesses of the new worker who soon packed his bags and left the church.

It is important that the same procedure for hiring a person be followed in releasing any member of the team. If the pastor chooses to release any team member on his own volition without a board decision, he no doubt will find himself in serious trouble with certain sympathetic friends of the team-person being released. No matter how gross the misconduct, someone will side with the person released.

The Senior Minister Becomes a Staff Enabler

In keeping with the servant/leader role, the senior minister will do all he can to see that each team member has a measure of success. He may not expect as much from each one as he does from himself, since they may not have the same years of experience, or the same drive or temperament. At weekly meetings and periodic planning retreats he will plan time for each team member to talk about his goals with the rest of the staff.

The pastor should encourage the church board to provide the

necessary resources and finances to see that the mission of each staff person is accomplished. He will encourage key persons in the local assembly to join the various staff members in accomplishing their particular objectives. He will provide time in the public meetings of the congregation to talk about the programs and ministry of each staff person. He will do everything to encourage the parents of the teens to attend the parent-teen quarterly meeting. He will make sure that each team member has equal time on the church master calendar, without scheduling or allowing other important meetings to be placed in conflicting time slots.

He will make periodic appearances at meetings scheduled by the various team members to show those who attend, as well as that particular team member, how really important each meeting is to him and to the whole team.

Peter McKnight was called as the new minister of Christian education for the State Street Church. He was told when he came to candidate that the church needed a stronger Sunday school. While candidating, Peter was assured that the Christian Education Board wished to make the space needed available in the building addition. The pastor gave lip service to the idea then, but he expected the next addition to the church facility to be a much enlarged office complex. Soon after Peter arrived on the job, group closure had set in on the adult department. The school, in his mind, had little chance of growth without new adult educational space. A vote for more space had little chance of passing without the full support of the senior pastor, who had gained much control during his eighteen years of tenure. Peter, like many team members, found himself with a great sense of frustration, because he wasn't provided the support and wherewithal to accomplish the task he believed the Lord wanted him to do.

The Senior Minister As Coordinator for Responsibilities

When a pastor works by himself, he knows that he oversees the entire ministry of the congregation. But when a church has a multiple staff, the senior pastor must work with the entire staff to see that the various goals of the congregation are being accomplished. The administration of the entire ministry becomes more complex as additional staff are added, because each phase of the ministry is assigned to a different person. A youth minister who does his task well will be working with the parents as well as the youth. Some ministers expect the youth pastor to provide all the necessary guidance for the families. Others don't even think about it, and still others want to shoulder that responsibility themselves. When this same church hires a Christian education director, the problem becomes even more complex, because the ministry to families becomes his major concern as well.

The chief of staff must see himself as the orchestrator of all the various ministries. He should realize that his ability is greatly enhanced through his team. Who is going to minister to the family and how can it best be done? A good team leader will guide the discussion of the team in thinking about where their church is going. Once decisions are made about how objectives will be accomplished, the chief of staff will follow up with periodic evaluations to see how well the decisions were implemented. On those occasions, readjustments in strategies and realignment of responsibilities may be made.

The senior pastor will not only orchestrate major ministry objectives, but also coordinate the week-by-week details of the church calendar. This will also include contacts or visits with members of the congregation. Someone needs to serve as the coach of the team to avoid loopholes and conflicts. Too often team members duplicate the activities of other team members because no one coordinated their areas of service.

Accountability is a significant part of the leader's responsibility in discipleship. Some leaders seem to feel that requiring accountability is an unpleasant task. Too often they forget that you honor a person by asking him to be accountable to someone.

When Pastor Jacobs asked Sam, the pastor of family ministries, to check into the possibility of using a campus facility for a summer family retreat, Sam immediately did his research. However, weeks went by and Pastor Jacobs never even as much as inquired about Sam's progress in finding a place. You can readily see how Sam felt about the request. If the pastor had checked on his progress the following week at the staff meeting, Sam would have felt that the pastor really cared about the retreat. If he cared enough to ask, Sam would have sensed that he was asked to do something significant. People are often indirectly saying, "I want to do something significant. You think I'm a worthy person because you asked me to do something that's worth my efforts."

No doubt that's part of the "provoking" process that the writer of Hebrews had in mind when he penned Hebrews 10:24 and 25 (KJV). When we come together as God's people, we ought to stimulate people in the body in ways that will help them produce love and good works. Give people a task to do that will challenge them because they see themselves being fulfilled in doing that mission. Then keep coming back to them to show that you care about their progress. In fact, you are so interested that you are anxious to help them in any way you can.

The Senior Minister As Truster and Supporter

Even though staff people ought to function as a staff, in reality they often only plan together, but do their work separately. Because of this, the trust level becomes significant. The same pattern follows in marriage. We have often seen that when trust is gone, the relationship turns into a divorce. When the church board or the senior pastor asks one of the staff people to turn in a report each day or week showing where he has spent his time, it is an indication of a crack in the trust level. Often this is precipitated by a low level of production, or a seemingly unwise use of time. It might also be rooted in envy on the part of the senior pastor. A great preventive step to avoid this is to concentrate on continually supporting one another. A flow of praise should go back and forth both privately and publicly between the team leader and team members. When the senior pastor praises the staff in public, you can count on the fact that there won't be political moves in the congregation to drive a wedge between staff members. The church people will see the strong sense of loyalty and trust.

It is especially important that the senior minister give recognition for his team's work, because much of what they do goes unnoticed by a majority of the congregation. The staff usually works behind the scenes, while the senior pastor has constant congregational exposure.

Each team member should treat a failure of another team member as he would his very own. He, furthermore, should never criticize his cohorts behind their backs. It must be obvious to the congregation that each team member recognizes that he lives within the Lord's redemptive context and is open and transparent about his sinful nature.

The pastor of discipleship and evangelism, Durk Johnstone, had what he considered to be a grand idea for evangelizing the neighborhood around the church. The staff discussion led to a reluctant approval. When the program failed, it would have been so easy to be critical. Instead, the senior pastor praised Durk for his creative effort. The team discussed what they could do differently next time to make it work. Durk was not discouraged to give it another try, and he also learned to listen to the team's advice. The team effort was strengthened by the whole experience. One of the leading laymen of the church paid the senior pastor a visit. He wanted to complain about the way Durk handled the special evangelistic service. Very wisely, the pastor took the blame for its failure and served as a buffer to Durk. Again, the team's unity was greatly enhanced in the eyes of the congregation.

The Senior Minister As Communicator

Counsellors suggest that 86% of American divorces are brought about by poor communication. We are convinced that the percentage would be similar in the breakdown of staff relationships.

A church staff in the Midwest followed an excellent daily practice of keeping the flow of communication wide open. At the close of each day they filled out an NCR (no carbon required) page listing their day's activities which, of course, included the names of people each team member had contacted that day. By doing this, no team member would find himself surprised about what was going on in the church family or programs.

No committee or board should meet without the rest of the staff seeing the agenda and minutes of those meetings. Here again, the senior pastor serves as the clearinghouse for all significant information. Nothing can so quickly destroy a team's harmony and trust level as the withholding of pertinent information. Of course, the larger the team, the more difficult it is to keep everyone informed.

The following study of communication breakdown in business shows the amount of communication that is heard and understood by persons in business firms and how it apparently diminishes between various levels of management.

President	90%
Vice President	67%
Department Director	50%
Foreman	30%
Non-manager Member	20%

(Source Unknown)

Lest this happens in church, everyone, but especially the senior pastor, must keep working on communication skills constantly. He has to be thinking all the time about seeing that everyone is informed, not only on the team, but in the congregation. Charles Ver Straten had a short section in his church's newspaper entitled, "Have You Heard?" This was a way to let everyone know, both what was going on and what was being contemplated. This opened the door for two-way communication, because it allowed others to express their feelings before a project got underway.

The Senior Minister As Pastor to the Staff

This role may appear to be the easiest assignment, because the minister is already serving as pastor. He often perceives his team to be accountable to him in a different way than the congregation, even though they are all part of the same body. A fine line exists between helping the staff as a nurturing discipler, and expecting productivity as a boss.

Jerry, a young, inexperienced youth pastor was on the team with a strong driving pastor, who had been a youth pastor himself at one time. When Jerry failed to live up to the expectations of some of the parents, the pastor brought him before the board for review. The board sent him back to work with a new list of expectations. He desperately needed a friend, a pastor, a discipler, who could guide and encourage him. Instead, he received a harder job description. Now his chance of success was slim. Many young men have potential which could be salvaged for a great ministry if only someone could see it in them, as Barnabas saw it in the newly converted Paul. Fortunately, after he was dismissed, another pastor saw that potential in Jerry and gave him a new chance.

When a minister becomes a pastor to his staff, he works on building a friendship with his team away from their church responsibilities. Russell Shive, chief of staff at Montavilla Baptist Church, became my friend on the golf course and over friendly lunches, where church business was set aside for the hour. Thus, our working relationship was strengthened when we were back at work.

Deep and meaningful times of prayer put the whole staff on an even footing before Christ, the real head of the church. The model small group prays as much for each other as they do for other members of the body.

The senior pastor serves as a model in life and ministry. The model is not a display of a perfect man, but of a saint on his pilgrimage toward spiritual maturity. He is just as quick to deal with his sins and failures as he is to show his Joshua-like ability to "stand fast in the Lord."

Project for Chapter 2

A. The Role of the Servant-style Leader

The first section of this chapter deals with the role of the servant-style leader and all its implications.

In keeping with what this chapter says on servant-style leadership, have each person choose another person on the team as a partner. Become fully aware of all the particulars about a task on which this person is currently working. Draw up a word picture of the ways he sees his teammate practicing servant-style leadership in that task. Include the communication, attitudes, and behavior to be practiced in the completion of the task. Now explain to that person how he can become a servant/leader in this particular situation.

B. The Role of the Team Leader

The second section of the chapter deals with the pastor's role as team leader.

The following project will take a secure leader and a considerate and loving staff, but it could be a tremendously helpful exercise in strengthening the teams' cooperation. It would be best if the senior pastor would initiate this project, since he is the one to be examined.

Have each team member mark on the scale where he sees the senior pastor currently functioning in relation to him. Now make a composite of each mark on each item. Use the composite as a springboard for discussion. Be sure to reinforce the senior pastor on his strengths first. Next talk about how you can help him overcome his weaknesses. It would be helpful if you conclude the session in prayer with each person giving an honest evaluation of how he can take steps to improve his own servant-style leadership.

1. A key role in the selection of the staff.

1	2	3	4	5	6
strong					weak

2. The senior minister becomes a staff enabler.

1	2	3	4	5	6
strong					weak

3. The senior minister as coordinator for responsibilities.

1	2	3	4	5	6
strong					weak

4. The senior minister as truster and supporter.

1	2	3	4	5	6
strong					weak

5. The senior minister as communicator.

1	2	3	4	5	6
strong					weak

6. The senior minister as pastor to the staff.

1	2	3	4	5	6
strong					weak

Part I: **Concerning the Team**

3

TEAMS MUST FACE THEIR PROBLEMS

"What makes you think I've got problems with my staff?"

3

TEAMS MUST FACE THEIR PROBLEMS

JAMES WROTE THAT a Christian should think twice about wanting to become a teacher. Gordon McDonald suggests, "You ought to think three times before leading or joining a staff. It is hard — delightful and rewarding if relationships are healthy, and destructive and disappointing if they are not."

We wouldn't warn you not to lead or join a staff anymore than we would discourage you from getting married. Chapter 1 should have whet your appetite for a team wedding. Just make sure you go in with your eyes wide open. In a sense, this book can serve as preparation for team work, just as a pre-marital book or course can prepare you for the bliss of marriage. As an adequate pre-marital course provides a section on the pitfalls of marriage, thus this chapter provides for the church team.

Many of the burgeoning population of singles could give scores of reasons for staying single. Working alone has advantages, too. Some have been alluded to in the earlier part of this book, but here are six major advantages to "singleness" that you should be aware of as you enter into a contractual arrangement with a team.

Singleness Is Better

1. The Over-Powering Personality

Senior Pastor Bob Lutz was a charismatic, powerful personality. It was no wonder that he found himself pastoring a large church with a staff of eight. Howard was approached as a candidate to be the associate. His main job description was to oversee and coordinate the other staff. Howard was a creative, strong people-oriented leader with a gift for administration. Pastor Bob was so assertive and dominant that Howard found himself smothered by Bob to the point that it was hard for him to lead. Many of the lay leadership were so taken up with the long-tenured senior pastor, that Howard lost any ambition to be creative.

Although you gain a rich, new perspective by the addition of a co-laborer, often certain parts of your personality may be smothered, and you may cease growing. It takes a great deal of honest communication on your part and a humble giving in on the part of other team members to prevent this from happening. The key is to find a person whose personality and leadership style will allow you to develop into the person you believe God wants you to be.

2. Unique Leadership Skills

Many people seeking staff positions have unique leadership skills. It is easy to find yourself on a team where you can't utilize that skill, because another person on the team is already assigned to that task. So not only will you find your personality smothered, but you will lose the opportunity to develop your leadership ability.

3. Church Philosophy

People trained primarily in a certain team context and church philosophy often have trouble fitting into the mold of another one.

Tom came up through the ranks of a large team in a California church. He was considered the star apparent for the head of the youth leadership team. A church of equal size and influence in Arizona invited him to head their youth leadership team. The week-long candidating process went well. Both sides asked what they thought to be all the right questions. During six months in his new position, the senior pastor put so much pressure on Tom to do things the pastor's way, that Tom left his new charge with a broken heart and a shattered self-image. (In a later section of this book we will provide some candidating guidelines which could prevent this problem.)

In talking with Tom, I found that although the words both churches used to describe their philosophy of ministry were the same, actually ministering at the Arizona church was quite different. Tom was so committed to his original training that he would not, could not, change.

4. Isolation

Alert leaders who work alone often feel their isolation and lack of input, so they tend to seek additional resources to expand their horizons. When a team joins hands and hearts in a venture, the members often fail to look outside their own circle for a broader world view. The danger is that the team will keep to themselves, and consequently lose a much-needed broader view of God's work in a world with a rapid-changing culture. We have seen individual churches, and sometimes whole denominations, become ineffective because of their lack of contact with the outside world.

Lyle Schaller calls large churches mini-denominations who face a strong temptation towards narcissism. They have all the staff and facilities to meet the needs of most of the people who come to their church. That tends to develop an ingrownness and self-love which becomes self-serving. Eventually that results in the feeling that God isn't even needed. The Psalmist warns us that we cannot build the church without Him. "Unless the Lord build the church, we labor in vain that build it."

5. Hiring Work Done

This next pitfall of team work is one of the most dangerous. It shows its ugly head more often than the others. No doubt we have become victims of our culture's influence, which suggests that we can pay to have any job done for us, if we can afford it. This is especially true of those people who were born in the '50s and later, and who find themselves in large congregations with corporate-level incomes.

Large churches have a dangerous tendency to hire people to do the ministry for them. It's easy for the staff people to fall into the same trap because they feel so much fulfillment in their ministry. It is rare to find a church where a large segment of the congregation sees the hiring of staff as a means of training and mobilizing the laity for ministry. But a powerful church results when the laity is genuinely released from maintenance-type tasks, is equipped through discipleship training, and then is mobilized for evangelism and nurturing-type ministries.

6. The Growing Church

Herman Sweet in *Multiple Church Staff* says of a small church, "While the pastor has a close personal relationship to most of his people, they will more readily tolerate mediocre preaching since they know him so well and accept him. They will fill in the gap. They listen and read between the lines. They know how much he does and they make excuses. But as the congregation grows, two factors loom larger — the first is that an ever-increasing percentage of the congregation must judge the pastor by his preaching because they do not have intimate contact with him in groups and in their homes." Other staff people have those contacts, and, in many cases, the people tend to respect them.

He goes on to say, "Second, and a more important reason, is that as the church grows larger and more complex, it needs more leaders and more money, and consequently, deeper motivation and the motive power are not there. In the last analysis the one greatest source of motive power for the church is an effective preaching of the Word, set in its proper setting of corporate worship. When the pastor obtains the assistant that he so desperately needs, he often finds it impossible to direct and measurably improve his preaching."

This appears to be another way the Peter Principle operates. The minister didn't choose to be elevated to the level of incompetency, the church did it to him without his knowing it. So a team is dangerous because it tends to put more responsibility on a person than he can handle. What is true of the preacher can readily happen to a staff person who can handle very nicely a group of twenty-five workers in the educational department, but will find a growing complexity of problems when he has to direct a staff of 250 people.

Potential Team Problems

Congratulations, you joined the team! You passed the test. You were able to see around all the apparent reasons not to join the team. But you aren't out of the woods yet. Working on a church staff is fraught with potential problems. Be aware of these problems so you can steer your route around them in your ministry pilgrimage.

1. Role and Title Misunderstandings

You won't get far into your dealing with the team before you run into some role and/or title misunderstandings. For those who have come to understand and appreciate diversity of function within unity, titles are not necessary. But for those who do not understand, the titles can be vastly misleading. Does a person who has the title of Minister of Christian Education mean that the pastor is not an educator or a teacher, or doesn't even see that as the very foundation of the church? You may even end up portraying the idea that the whole church doesn't teach. Many churches have tried to deal with this problem by suggesting that each staff person is a minister. A minister of music, a minister of youth, and so on. But even those titles have problems, so other churches have done away with the definitive part of the title and have simply called each person a minister. However, you may need to face reality and use the title, because the parishioner doesn't comprehend that nomenclature and will give team members titles according to the way one sees them functioning.

You can take various steps to help the congregation more readily see the team members as equals, although there is no way this can be totally accomplished. As each team member preaches, leads in worship, does such other pastoral tasks as visiting, leading in the ordinances, and heading up certain committees, mutual respect will result. The pastor, who serves as chief of staff, will play a major role as he constantly makes reference to his fellow ministers and avoids "my church" kind of comments.

A simple exercise can develop a better feeling about these titles and roles, and will aid the staff and the church boards. Give each person a blank piece of paper and ask each one to draw one circle on the page for each staff member. Have each one give particular attention to the size of the circle, any overlapping of the circles, and the relationship each one has to the other. Then discuss the differences in the diagrams. This could be done with real profit at a staff retreat or when a new member joins the team. Here are a couple of sample diagrams.

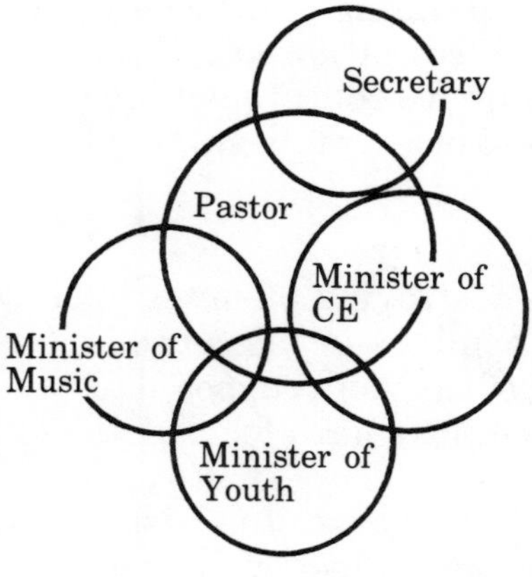

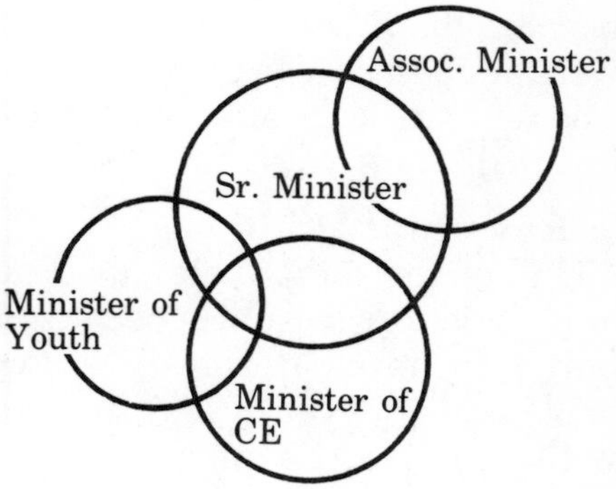

This will no doubt help to bring into the open any misconceptions and false expectations about roles.

A major unresolved agenda item for many evangelical churches and denominations is how to handle women who feel a strong call to ministry and display talents often superior to male members of the clergy. Some churches can readily give the title of Director to a woman who ministers in the role of Christian education, but never grant her the title of Minister of Christian Education because the role or title of minister or elder is given only to men in the Scriptures.

Dealing with the title, Assistant to the Minister, or Associate, can prove a problem to those who carry the title, but it seldom seems to make much difference to the congregation. In general, Associate tends to carry the connotation of equality, while the title of Assistant leaves the image of one who assists the senior pastor in carrying out his task. The congregation is far more interested in the person's depth of life, and style of ministry, than in the title the staff person bears.

There seems to be a constant flux in the use of titles. Directors of Christian education and assistant pastors were some of the first persons added to the staff. In recent years the title Minister of Christian Education has taken on a couple of new cloaks. One is Minister of the Family, another is Minister of Discipleship and Evangelism. A true Minister of Christian Education was always in charge of ministering to the family, and should have always been training people in discipleship, and guiding the church in its evangelistic ministry. Too many ministers became paper pushers and desk-style administrators, and failed to minister to families, guide the church in its evangelism, and make its teaching really disciple-building. Many churches became disillusioned with Christian education and those who were supposed to be directing the church's educational program. The new titles are simply new titles to older ministers that failed to fulfill their expectations.

2. Envy and Pride

One of the most insidious, team-destroying enemies is envy and pride. It's so subtle because it's hidden in the subconscious part of the mind. Besides, a servant of God isn't supposed to have pride and so, even if it is discovered, it is hard for him to deal with it out in the open.

If a pastor has served alone in all his years of ministry, and suddenly finds himself having a second staff person, he may find it hard to share the limelight. It is hard to be honest with himself if he feels threatened by a new staff person, who is apparently having greater success than he is. His envy may express itself by asking his associate to carry his briefcase up the stairs.

When Pastor Anderson went away on vacation and then on to his denominational yearly meetings, he asked the new young associate, Jim Short, to preach for him. When he came home, numerous members of the congregation reported to their pastor with a delight the outstanding sermons their new associate preached. Most of those who sang his praises were quick to emphasize that they would like him to preach more often. They never gave any thought to how this might hurt Pastor Anderson. He thought, "Well, don't they enjoy my preaching anymore? After all, I'm better trained and have had many more years of experience than he has." He mused even further, "It must be that those people don't like me exposing their sins through my strong biblical preaching. They'll get accustomed to him soon, just as they have to me."

When the church board had approached Mr. Anderson two years before about getting an associate, their rationale for hiring a second man was based on his heavy work load. He received it as a compliment then, but the truth was that they saw him as unable to attract the younger crowd. They thought a more youthful associate could do that better. His inability to deal with his pride now only tended to build a wall in his mind against his new team member, Jim Short. He became critical of Jim as he went about his tasks. This was his way of getting even with Jim for stealing his admirers.

Every new team member will gather the affection of some of the congregation — those who were fond admirers of another team member. The attraction may be his administrative skills, his warm personality, his lovely family, his ability to show genuine concern for others. If those potential matters of pride are not dealt with in each staff member's heart when a new member arrives, he can quickly find himself blocking the door to effective cooperation. Even confessing his pride to the team will help him get it out of the involuntary side of his mind and deal with it in an honest and open fashion. After all, isn't that what he expects the congregation to do with their pride?

Pastor Earl found a mature way to deal with the same problem. Clark came to Christ under Earl's ministry some years before. He ultimately went on to seminary and then served as Earl's youth pastor. As the church grew and as Clark's strengths in preaching became more apparent, Pastor Earl encouraged him to become his associate. In another year the congregation decided to take a step of faith and started a daughter congregation. It was obvious from the start that Clark was God's man for the new work. Pastor Earl supported him all the way. He was honest enough to admit that he was envious of losing all those young people to Clark's church. About one hundred young adults made the move, with the full blessing of the mother church. Instead of cringing in fear, Pastor Earl led the mother church to move out in faith. Within a year the daughter church was growing and healthy, and the mother church was averaging more people than it had before the new church got underway.

3. Failure to Be Open

That leads us to another potential spiritual problem. If *koinonia* is going to be a part of a team's experience, each member must practice transparency and openness. There can be no agendas, no defensiveness, and no anxieties hidden from the open view of the team. Each person will block the team, either from communication, or from a genuine owning of their common goal, if he is not transparent.

Unbeknown to the other four members of a staff in a well-known and highly respected metropolitan church of 1,000 members, one of their team was having serious marital problems. It's easy to understand that his pride kept him from sharing this with the rest of the team. He took out his feelings of frustration and hostility on the senior pastor at many church staff meetings. He disagreed with him on major issues and was able to rally the other three second-level staff members against their pastoral leader. Just before the whole frustrating situation blew up, the marital problem ended in divorce and the man left the church. If he had only shared his problem with those team members at the time, he may have found his marriage saved and the whole cause of Christ spared another setback. Each member of a miniature body of Christ needs to share all his hurts and frustrations so the team can reach out and minister to them. The team meeting which we will discuss later will more fully show how to deal with this.

4. Failure to Communicate

One of the beautiful things about the body of Christ is that we can communicate about life's richest experiences. We do it in sermons, testimonies, singing, prayer times, conversations in covenant groups, and discussions about the Scriptures. Our church experiences are rated in proportion to the level of the depth of communication that we sense. Isn't marriage also rated the same way? What about the church staff? Communication is probably on the top of the list of the items that either make or break a staff's effectiveness. If a congregation senses that godly communication is going on among the staff, they will envy and try to emulate what they see modeled.

Numerous volumes have been written about the art and pitfalls of communication. Since lack of it is no doubt one of the major causes of staff infection, we will at least deal with it here. We will also address it more fully in Part II.

The difficulty in communication is in proportion to the number of staff members. The addition of each staff member increases the combination of relationships in a geometric pattern. A staff of eight and their spouses enlarges the relations into the thousands of combinations. It's amazing that we do as well as we do in our communications. Here are some of those enemies that peck away at our communication efforts on our church staffs.

a) *Assumptions* — Memos, phone calls, written job descriptions, and policy guidelines are seldom meaningful in curing communication breakdowns. Face-to-face meetings in any kind of setting are the best way to overcome communication gaps. When we tend to assume that others know what is going on, that they know what we are thinking and what we want from them, then the bubble of frustration comes to the breaking point. I am constantly amazed to hear staff members complain about other staff members because they failed to do a certain thing or comment on a certain subject. But when I ask them if they have ever told the others what their expectations are, they shamefully confess that they either didn't dare to or never got around to do it.

b) *Hidden Agenda* — We play games in the church quicker than any other place because we have higher expectations of each other than most people and organizations. Consequently, we are reticent to tell what we really want or expect.

Jerry deeply wanted to be the speaker at the couples' conference but was hesitant to let on, for fear the staff would think he was pushing himself on the group. As he led the discussion in the staff meeting, the rest of the team voted for a local marriage counsellor to take the assignment. His agenda was defeated and he had to work out his resentment toward the other team members. What was even harder now was that he had a difficult time encouraging the church couples to attend the conference. If their team had been a place where feelings were easily expressed and everyone trusted the others, Jerry could have talked openly about what he wanted.

When a team begins to have its *real* meeting out in the hall after the called meeting, it is time to even out the kinks in communicating honest differences.

c) *Language* — Our words don't have meaning; we mean the words, but the listeners have a different way of translating those words through their unique filters. We need to keep checking to see exactly what the other person said. Don't forget the body language that is made up of touch, movement, stances, and the intentions of our symbols.

It may surprise you when you realize that our messages are made up of three components.

Content	7%
Tone	38%
Non-Verbal	55%

If the components don't agree in what they communicate, they will have a hard time communicating.

The University Church of a western city had a staff of senior pastor, youth pastor, and a man whose job description called upon him to cover Christian education and church administration. The church was flourishing under their leadership. A consultant studied the Christian education program and recommended that the CE program could use a person giving his full time to it. The pastor chose to take the administrative task and asked the other men to spend all of their energies on the CE program. He found the courage to talk in a frank, sweet spirit with the educational pastor about his dissatisfication with the leadership he was giving the educational ministry. The pastor communicated clearly just what he expected. The educational pastor was greatly relieved to learn that he could concentrate totally in one area and to know just what would be expected of him. The pastor testified that he had little confidence that this would make the difference in his leadership skills or that the Christian education program would flourish under his leadership. One year later, he related to the consultant and the minister of Christian education his pleasure at the great maturity and skill his educational pastor had developed during that year. While the pastor had been ready to dismiss him earlier, now he confessed that he was his most valuable asset. Without a continual flow of honest communication, a life and maybe a whole church would have been torn asunder.

d) *Defensiveness* — Pastor Howard moved from Illinois to a southwestern church where Donald had already served for five years as youth minister. Donald knew the congregation well. He understood the open mindset of the congregation far better than Howard. However, Howard had ministered for over twenty-five years and believed that he could lead the congregation very well. Before the first year had passed, a large segment of the congregation resisted Howard's conservative midwestern style of worship and leadership. Even though Donald was twenty years younger, he knew what the people needed and expected. If Howard was to hear the messages communicated, he would need to change. He didn't see it as enhancing his life or ministry. Young Donald didn't know how to honestly affirm and encourage his elder pastor, so this built the defensive mechanism even more. The impasse in their communication had grown so strong that staff meetings were no longer held. Soon the whole congregation sensed the tension which was building. Defensiveness, which is a form of closure, tends to shut off any significant input about how he could minister effectively. Anyone, young or old, finds himself defensive if his self-image is so weak that he can't listen to advice from another team member.

5. Failure to Stand in Another's Shoes

Matthew 7:1 suggests that we should never judge another because we don't really want justice, and because we can't see the other person's perspective. Most of the time, because of our own failures and shortcomings, we don't see things from someone else's viewpoint. It takes a lot of honest patience to see life through another person's lenses, or feel what it is like to walk in another's moccasins.

Steve, a young part-time youth minister, portrayed this better than any older person could ever be expected to do. His pastor had served as a foreign missionary for over twenty-five years. His godly zeal for his congregation was often clouded by the influence of another culture. Numerous members of the congregation complained to Steve, with an urgent request for him to do something about the pastor's failure in the pulpit. It would have been easy for Steve to side with them because he too saw the pastor's weakness. Instead, he challenged them to join him at the church each Saturday night for a prayer meeting. Many took up his challenge and they beseeched God that He would pour down His blessings on their pastor and their congregation. God answered their prayers in a marvelous way. Many people came to Christ for salvation, the church grew, and the pastor became a great preacher. Of course, that team grew as a genuine model of how the body ought to accept and help each other grow.

The Johari Window[1] is a good way to picture the long, tedious process of identifying with another person.

Box I	Information known to all of us
Box II	Blind to you, but known by others
Box III	Blind to others, but known by you
Box IV	Blind to all of us (unknown activity area; future of "us"?)

When the team *begins*, it looks something like this:

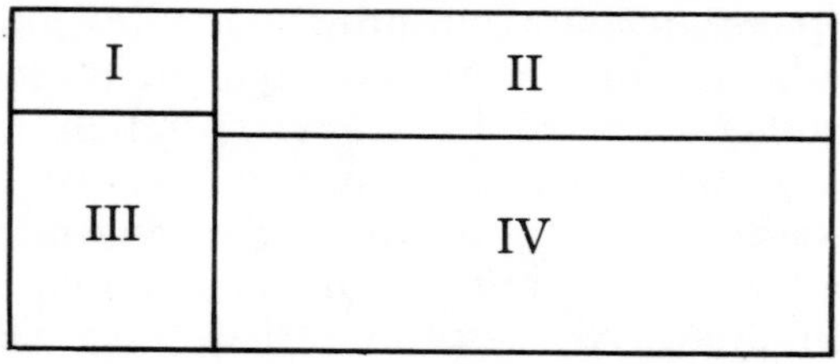

Three years from now, we hope it will look like this:

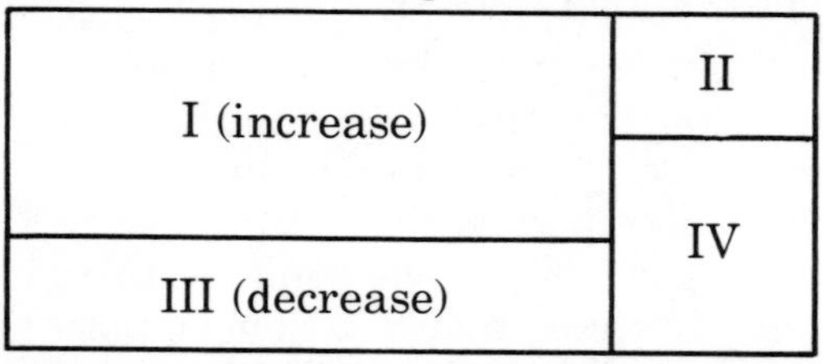

When we start out cold (all of us new to one another) or semicold (some of us know one another), let's fight assumptions. Admit that we actually need to know much more about us. *The Johari Window* is a good prop or X-ray of how much we're aware of at the start of being a team. And how we *want* to look in awareness of each other at the finish (three years from now when we're rolling?).

Our *goal* becomes enlarging Box I, what we all know, and decreasing Boxes II and III, hidden areas. Box IV will always be an area of consideration, but it, too, can be reduced through the illuminator-lubricator called The Johari Window: An X-ray for Awareness: How much do we know?

A lot of factors influence this perception, but it starts when all the team members have a strong desire to understand the other person's perspective. If one staff member's maturity, the extent of his education, and his perceptual skills exceed that of other staff members, then he will need to be far more tolerant of other team members who are slower to gain the complete picture on a given issue.

6. Defective Covenants

Written job descriptions are no more a guarantee that teams will work together well than marriage certificates will guarantee a happy and successful marriage. When members of a staff come together, they agree to certain working arrangements. Whether they are on paper or not doesn't guarantee their effectiveness. The thing that counts most is the worth of the person's commitment to keep covenants. The Apostle James wisely reminds us that our years ought to be an unchanging commitment to our word. Closely related to the religious idea of a covenant is the legal idea of a contract. Wayne Oats says, "Probably the basic factor in all human relationships, effective or ineffective, is that of the covenants that band the people involved into relationships to one another. This idea of covenants is vital to the biblical view of our relationship to God. The covenant becomes the basis of appeal in human relationships."

When Delbert began to work as the youth pastor with Pastor Dean, they had seriously discussed their philosophy of ministry and their stewardship of time. They had agreed that their family should receive a strong emphasis in their weekly schedule. Dean would spend more time with the ministry, since Delbert would be finishing his seminary degree. A year or so into the working relationship, Pastor Dean criticized Delbert for spending only about forty hours at the church, while Dean was spending about seventy hours in church-related business. You can almost hear the phrases coming out of their conversation, "When I came here, you said that . . . ," or, "I thought we had that straight, but. . . ."

This idea of an agreed-upon covenant doesn't mean that it cannot be changed. The story of the Old Testament is the dramatic account of how God made new covenants with His people. In the New Testament, we see Christ giving His people a new covenant. In the same way, these two men in the account at hand could have worked out a new covenant. But at this point, as in the beginning, the terms must be agreeable to both parties. A covenant is a dynamic, flowing, changing reality, but communication must be open constantly between the partners. This is a reflection of their mature sensitivity to the work of the Holy Spirit.

Louis Evans, Jr., has forged out eight principles of a covenant which he has used as a common agreement between covenant-style groups. It would be helpful for a church staff to build its working relationships upon this covenant. It serves as a reminder of the kind and type of relationship we intend to maintain as a team. It's important, therefore, that it be brought out periodically for discussion and evaluation. The following eight principles from his book *Covenant to Care* are not quotes but summary statements:

a) *The Covenant of Affirmation* — Agape Love.
"I will love you and affirm you no matter what you have said or done. I love you as you are and for what Christ wants to make of you."

b) *The Covenant of Availability*
"Anything I have — time, energy, wisdom, myself, finances — are all at your disposal. I give these to you and the covenant group in a unique way."

c) *The Covenant of Regularity*
"I covenant to give a regular part of my time to this group when it decides to meet. I consider that time to be of highest priority on my schedule."

d) *The Covenant Prayer*
"I promise to pray for you, to uphold you, and to attempt to be sensitive to the Holy Spirit concerning your needs."

e) *The Covenant of Openness*
"I will show myself to you, letting you know who I am as a person in feeling, history, hopes, and hurts; in other words, I will need you!"

f) *The Covenant of Honesty*
"I will be honest in my mirroring back to you what I sense and feel coming from you."

g) *The Covenant of Confidentiality*
"What goes on in this group stays here. I will say nothing that may be traced back or that could be injurious or embarrassing to my covenant partners."

h) *The Covenant of Accountability*
"You have a right to expect growth from me so that I may give you the fullness of the gifts which God has bestowed upon me and fulfill my God-created designs. Therefore I will not languish in the process of growth."

7. Power vs. Authority

"John, it looks as if we can't work on the same team anymore. Either you will have to leave or I will. Our philosophy of ministry is too different, and it looks as if they will never mesh."

"You can see, Don, that our lack of facilities is going to cut off our growth. I'm asking you to give high priority in the next six months to organizing a task force to solve this problem. This is going to be necessary even though you don't like the assignment, and even though it means changing the emphasis of your ministry for these six months."

"I'm calling a meeting Friday evening of all the people who have complained about your leadership in our church's youth program. I want you to work out a reasonable solution with the parents. You may find yourself extremely hurt and perhaps you are going to feel defensive, but if you don't come to an agreeable solution you may find yourself without a job."

"Pastor, in the last three months my wife and I have had twelve families tell us of their dissatisfaction with your lack of leadership in our church. Are you aware of their feelings? I'm concerned that many of them will leave if some changes aren't made. I think I can help if you are interested."

Each of these stories could be repeated a thousand times in various forms each week in American churches. You can readily see that each has serious consequences. Tension is building in each one, and the future success or failure of each ministry hangs in the balance. Most of the other pitfalls mentioned in this chapter are also part of each scenario, but the major issue they have in common is a struggle over the use of and response to authority and power.

When ministers join hands and hearts together in a team, they will constantly be facing significant issues. The amount of success they experience will be related to the way each person on the team deals with authority. Who has it? How did he get it? How does he use it? What are the motives that are behind the way he uses it, and how others perceive and respond to his use of it? It is critical that each person understand the lines of authority when he joins the team. Even though they are clarified verbally and in writing at the outset, this doesn't guarantee that they will always function that way. Every new agenda may change each person's perception of power. Nonetheless, it is critical that they be clarified at the outset.

Mary never questioned that Pastor Robin was the leader of the team. But at a weekly staff meeting, Pastor Robin announced that they would no longer use their denominational publishing house's Sunday school curriculum, because of its loose stance on the inspiration of Scripture. Since Mary was the Director of Christian Education and she was given the supervision of the Sunday school, she assumed that any matter pertaining to the curriculum was under her authority. The pastor saw this as a greater issue since it related to the theological position that the church took and its relationship to their denomination. This issue was never even contemplated when Mary was hired. Why wasn't she consulted before the decision was made? It was time not only to discuss the curriculum, but a time for both of them to be honest about their feelings. Even though Pastor Robin thought he had the right to make such a decision, he took unfair advantage of Mary and her authority. It was time for him to ask Mary's forgiveness, and then to talk through the issue of the curriculum.

Larry Richards in his book *Youth Ministry* suggests that there are three kinds of leadership, each of which expresses a different type of authority. First, there is coercive power. Most often this is used to manipulate team members without explicity telling them what is wanted. Pastor Robin was guilty of doing this. There are few occasions when this kind of power should be used. "Coercive power is exercised when laws, rules, and regulations are stated, and the person under authority is to respond to them. When laws and rules are broken, power to punish or enforce behavior is exercised, again in an essentially impersonal way."[2] A senior pastor who is insecure will often operate this way.

"Another base for authority is seen in the institutional role. Here persons are organized together for the accomplishment of some purpose, and to better achieve that goal, different functions are assigned to specific persons. Each of these people have certain powers to reward or punish behavior that aid or inhibit the reaching of organizational goals."[3] There are more occasions when this style of authority is displayed in a church staff than when coercive power is used, but it certainly is not desirable either.

"A third type of authority is provided by ability. Because a person is recognized by others to have a special degree of competence, they follow his lead. The authority which I've described as ability-based exists only in the context of relatively close interpersonal relationships. Only when ability and competence are demonstrated, and the endurance of competence is maintained through continued contact, will an ability-based authority produce a conformity that is characterized by an inner desire to respond."[4] It is beautiful to see a lead pastor demonstrate this balance of skill in leadership and love for his team.

8. Failure to Commonize

Each team member needs to have his own special assignment and responsibility. He needs to do his task with all the energy and ability he can muster. However, if he fails to be interested in what the other team members are doing, and even be unwilling at times to step across his lines of responsibility and participate in the other team members' ministries, deep resentment can build up.

It is easy for the senior pastor to expect each staff member to aid him in the worship service, but he may be reluctant to make a contribution to what he considers to be less significant. "You help me lead in the worship service, but I don't have time to go along with you on the youth retreat this time." You might also hear this song played in reverse, "I'm too busy doing the youth ministry to help you in the hospital calling this week, Pastor."

On a large team it becomes increasingly difficult to engage in commonizing ministries, but at least every effort should be made to be deeply interested in other ministries. Only when each member takes an occasion to cross the lines periodically will a genuine team spirit develop.

Project for Chapter 3

Dealing With Staff Infection

Chapter 3 deals with the eight problems which most often cause staff infection. Here is one meaningful way you can prevent these diseases from occurring, or help cure them if you are infected with them. This project can be used during a staff meeting or staff retreat.

A. Ask each staff member to read the chapter seeking to identify any of the diseases related to your staff.
B. At a time when all the team members are together, have each one in turn identify a disease which is true of the team's relationship, current or in the past. Review as many details of scenario as deemed necessary.
C. Seek to discuss openly the way the situation was handled. Keep in mind that it is just as helpful to talk about situations that were handled properly as it is to talk about ones that were handled improperly.
D. Deal with any feelings, attitudes, or need to seek forgiveness for improper judgments or actions.
E. Spend time praying that the Lord will grant strength to function as a genuine microcosm of the body of Christ.

Part II: **The Functioning of a Team**

4

MAINTAINING A BALANCED TEAM

© Erik Johnson

"I'll preach on Thanksgiving, Christmas, New Year's and Easter. You can have 'The Role of Women in the Church,' 'Tongues Speaking for Today,' 'Biblical Inerrancy,' and our special 'Fund Drive Sunday.' "

4

MAINTAINING A BALANCED TEAM

"WE ALL HAVE equal rights and worth" has been the big cry coming out of the fire and smoke of the "rights" movement thundering through American society the last few decades. For the most part, the evangelical church has been in agreement with the sentiment of the movement. It had some roots in our Constitution, but its complete picture goes back to Genesis, to Christ's teaching in the Gospels, and to the Epistles.

I'm grateful that God gave me a wife to complete what I did not have in my own nature (Gen. 2:18). A family can hardly handle one father; what in the world would we do with two? Romans 12 and 1 Corinthians 12 both stress the need for believers to work hard on recognizing the diversity in the body. I gather the impression that some folks believe we ought to do this because we all came out of the cookie cutter looking different. You missed it if that is what you believe. God made us all uniquely different because the church couldn't serve each other, or reach the world, without that diversity of skills.

Many ingredients are needed to accomplish a ministry. Paul implies this in Ephesians 4:10-12 when he tells the church that Christ gave them His ascension gifts so they could direct or administrate ("equip") the spiritual work of the church.

Any administrative event breaks naturally into *four parts*. The first one has to do with ideas or *concepts*. The second has to do with *things*, or the operation of the event. The third and fourth have to do with *people*. People need someone to excite and encourage them to become involved in the work of God. Once the event is launched, someone needs to be concerned for the human relationships which revolve around that event.

A genuine Christ-style servant/leader must be deeply committed to dealing with all three elements: concepts, things, and people. He will be ineffective in his ministry if he neglects to deal with any one of the elements. He'll be equally foolish if he thinks that any one of them is less important than another. The seed of descent and decay of a team lies right here. Caring for all the areas is what is conceived of as a wholistic ministry.

Christ as our model servant/leader demonstrated this many times. For example, He sent out the Twelve to witness in Matthew 10. The whole theological meaning of the church lies behind the idea of them going out and delivering the message. The redemption of mankind and the building of the church was inherent in their going. Jesus gave much emphasis to the event. He told the disciples whom they were to address and how they were to address them. He added some words about their personal wellbeing. Notice also the great concern for their relationship with each other, and the motivation for this concern. Here is the motivation. "The kingdom of heaven is at hand." Watch the negotiating. "Whoever does not receive you . . . shake off the dust of your feet" (Matt. 10:14). The whole chapter is replete with *a balance of these three* ingredients. You'll see the same thing each time the Lord is displaying His servant/leadership role. Many ministry events of churches fail because the leadership is unbalanced in its approach. The leaders either think that one of the three elements is not essential, or they simply overlook one of them.

Read very carefully now. Here is the major thesis of this book. Few, if any, people have outstanding skills in all four styles of leadership. This is why teams are necessary. When the church tackles an event, someone has to give leadership to all four elements. If you have one or more persons with a special skill in each area, the event will have its greatest impact.

It is fascinating to hear Jesus give titles to those who work in His kingdom. You will note, on the diagram that follows, how the four titles He uses reveal the work of those four tasks. The *prophet-seer* is the man of God who deals with theology, philosophy, and rational thinking. He is God's agent who communicates the truth and the vision of the kingdom. He analyzes the need of society and applies theology to the need.

The *steward* is the operational manager who makes sure the vineyard is properly cared for so it will be most productive. There is no wasted energy, seed, or fruit. He sees that everyone is doing his task in the proper sequence so that the harvest will produce a hundred-fold. But take note that it's the seed of the prophet that is planted and which will produce. Yet if you have seed, you must have someone to guard its growth. As the steward studies God's vineyard, he makes decisions and then expedites the application of that theology.

People are the central focus of God's kingdom (note that the largest section has to do with people) and He sends two of His ambassadors to relate to them. It's the apostle or herald who communicates the theology. He tells God's people how they can work in the vineyard and receive a hundred-fold for their labors. Their lives will be rich when they take an active part in the kingdom of God. He keeps saying, "Blessed are you" (or, you'll be completed), when you are "poor in spirit," "hunger and thirst after righteousness," or become "pure in heart." "Come and follow Jesus," the prophet says. And Jesus promises, "When you do all that I commanded you, then I'll reveal Myself to you."

Last we come to the command to *God's workers* (1 Pet. 5:2 NIV). "Be shepherds of God's flock that is under your care." Anyone who has served as a shepherd knows how urgently God's people need a shepherd. They go their own way, do their own thing, and get entangled with one another so that the work of God sometimes takes steps backward. The shepherd is needed to listen to their bleeding hearts, bring reconciliation to schisms among the sheep, and motivate them to once again enter God's vineyard to do God's theology.

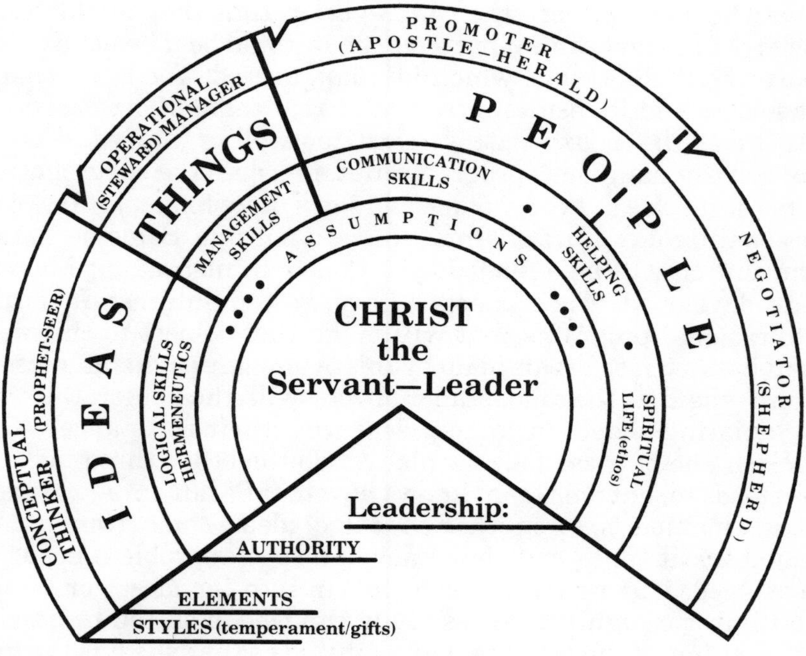

Now that we've looked at the theoretical side of the team, let's see how this is worked out in the church.

At the First Baptist Church, the Associate Pastor, Marvin, has a job description that calls for him to concentrate on discipleship and evangelism. He faces the need to equip the saints so that he can duplicate himself. He conceived a plan to equip the members of the church for all the leadership roles needed. He envisions in his mind how a special training program ought to be structured. He not only can conceive of the idea, but he can put it on paper; so the whole team has the overall outline. The *problem* is how will he launch the program?

Thank the Lord! He has given Judy to the team. As a Christian Education Director she has the skills of an operational manager. She has a good picture of all the little details that Marvin couldn't envision in his mind. She also has the discipline common to a steward or operational manager. She'll see to it that the school operates smoothly and, because of her care, the school will continue to operate year after year.

Neither Judy nor Marvin can inspire people when they get in front of crowds. Pastor Lewis stirs a crowd when he preaches. He is a real motivator. He does it in his preaching, and he's the one who can convince the congregation that they ought to be a part of the program. What a shame it would be if he got excited only about the things which he inaugurated! Too often that's the case, and it results in a lack of real team effort.

John is the Youth Pastor — not too well organized, doesn't conceive of many new programs, but, my, does the congregation love him! He's every older person's adopted son. He can desensitize a conflict of almost any magnitude. Some people in the church will be offended by this new ministry that Marvin has developed. These people have vested interest in other educational programs that will make them object to this new harebrained idea dreamed up by this over-aggressive staff person. John is sent as the ambassador of good will, the healer, the true negotiating shepherd to help deal with their resistance.

Each one of these four people can do the other three tasks if he needs to, but this team knows how to take advantage of each team member's strengths. Creative ideas come from other members at times, but they know if a special problem needs to be solved, it is better to send Marvin into the closet or woods to think through the issues. Judy can't be expected to handle everything. If the other team members see that she has the gift of administration, they will call on her to get their particular tasks organized too. Envy and pride should not exist if each one comprehends his gifts or temperament style, and realizes that each person has received his own gift from the Spirit.

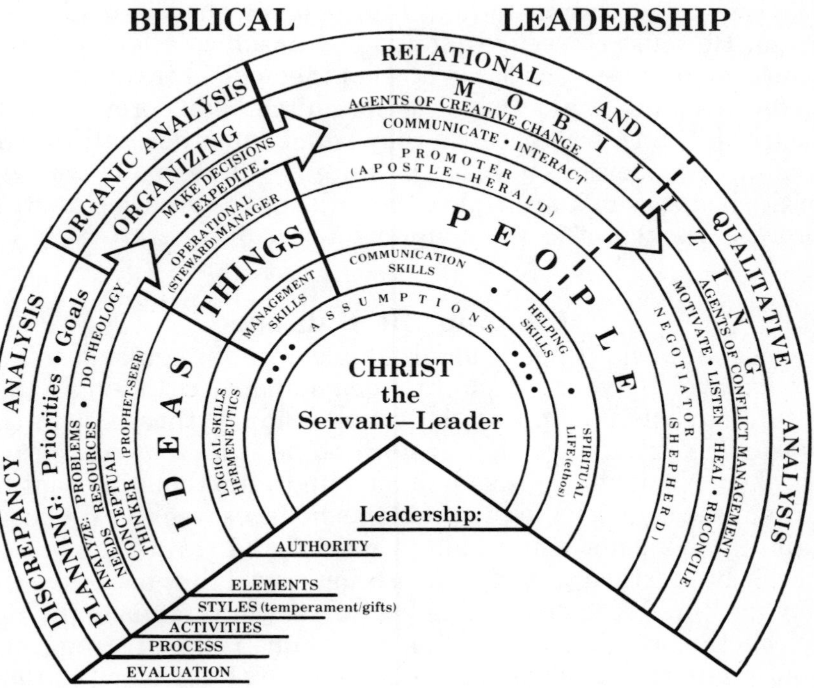

Adding Team Members

If you buy this theory of a team, it will greatly influence the way you approach adding new team members. At the end of the chapter you will find Myron Rush's "Management Temperament Analysis Test." You can discover what the greatest strength of each team member is by using this instrument. You have taken a necessary first step in choosing your next staff member once you have seen the balance of the team. After each team member takes the test and you analyze its accuracy, you may determine that you are missing an operational manager on the team. Rather than hiring an associate just to supervise certain ministries, you should also look for a candidate who knows about those special ministries and also has the temperament necessary to aid the team as an operational steward. This test is helpful because it makes an objective judgment of the person.

A pastor who works alone is limited, because he can't master a total balanced ministry by himself. Only Christ could do that. The pastor will be a wise leader if he calls on the elders and other leaders in the church to help him balance out the leadership team. He must be secure enough in himself to allow a person who may not have the same level of theological training to aid in directing the total ministry of the church. Many proud pastors nearly kill a church because they won't tap other willing and available leadership to bring balance to the team. This is one of the beauties of a multiple elder rule, or the creative staffing process, spoken of in the chapter on recruiting staff.

Keeping the Balance

Once an obvious operational manager on a team said to me, "Whenever I give my pastor an idea on paper with a plan that would obviously help him, he sets it aside or throws it in the wastebasket." I know that pastor and he is a great conceptual thinker. No doubt he is so wrapped up in his thoughts that he cannot see solutions to the problems he faces weekly. He keeps talking about not being able to recruit and train the staff he needs, but he throws away the precious jewel that may save the day for him. He keeps calling his fellow workers his team, but rejects the practice of operating as a team. You will strengthen your ministry and honor your team members by drawing on their God-given insight and talent. It's amazing how this process opens up two-way communication.

Up to this point it may sound like a simple process. All four kinds of people do their thing and, like a flash, you are successful. Sorry, but it isn't that easy. There are other factors to keep in mind.

Pastor Grawman built the Elm Street church from a home Bible study to a thriving congregation of 300 in a period of five years. The newly appointed search committee settled on a promising young seminarian for their first associate. He had been the student body president and had won the preaching award at his denominational seminary. But like many bright-eyed seminarians, Mark hadn't had much experience. His mind was filled with many idealistic ideas. He marked high on the conceptual side of the graph.

Pastor Grawman was in his late forties and had proven that he knew how to lead. He had worked out his philosophy of ministry on the grindstone of experience. He knew he was a strong negotiating manager and needed someone to help create new concepts for his church. The natural rapid growth, which they had enjoyed since the church's inception, had now leveled off.

Friction set in before many months had passed. Mark presented his grand ideas to his pastor, but Grawman knew they wouldn't work. He had tried them before, or seen another church fall on its face while working its way through those programs. Mark and his pastor were ready to give up trying to work as a team. Age and lack of experience met head-on. They needed to learn to practice dialogue wherein each one would honestly listen to the other and be open about his own feelings. They needed to learn to respect each other's ideas and opinions. Pastor Grawman needed to give Mark a chance to try his ideas, and maybe even to fail. The pastor's maturity could reshape Mark's ideas to be more acceptable and useful to both of them.

At Bethel Church Pastor George Thompson built his ministry because of his warm shepherd's heart. He challenged people with his enthusiastic preaching. He spent much time in home visitation and in counselling. It was a common occurrence to find the other two staff members in the church office waiting for George to show up for their scheduled staff meeting. He was often an hour late because he couldn't leave the person he was counselling. He seldom had time to talk about the church program. He would say, "You men just go ahead and run the program and I'll deal with the people." He showed little or no respect for his team members, who had keen insight about ways he wouldn't have to work so hard and could still meet the people's spiritual needs.

Usually a person's temperament strengths are his greatest love. He doesn't want anyone organizing him out of this love. Teamwork will tend to reveal one's weaknesses. George's love for people and his ability to relate to them was obviously his greatest strength. That great love for his people became such a strong drive that he failed to see the other elements of the ministry. He failed to see that he needed to duplicate that love in others. He didn't realize that this could be done. If he had let his team help him structure a program to recruit and train others to do what he was doing, he would have ultimately enriched many other people.

Myron Rush's diagram from his book, *Management: A Biblical Approach*, shows how Bethel Church could have prospered from a true team approach.

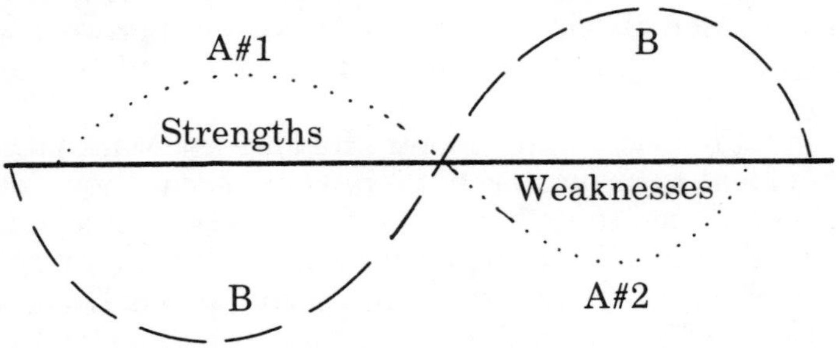

Pastor George's strength (relational skills) is shown in character A#1 and his weakness (inability to structure a training program to equip people in relational skills) is shown in A#2. He needed another one of his team (B), with opposite strengths and weaknesses, to fortify his ministry. He felt that if they worked together, he would have to give up his love for people. In actual fact, his team members could help him use his love and strength to an even greater extent if they would work together in loving and equipping people to love each other.

I agree with Rush that many lead pastors like George see their other staff members as having failed in their ministry because they do not have the same strengths and commitments. So these pastors attempt to correct those weaknesses, or even fire the staff members. The dotted line on the diagram illustrates George's effort to correct his own and his team's weaknesses. By using certain motivational methods, you can actually correct some of those weaknesses. The trouble with this, however, is that you, in addition to eliminating some of the weaknesses, also eliminate some of the strengths. Rush suggests that by concentrating on one's strengths, and finding a team member with opposite strengths to complete the leadership cycle, one can build a much stronger team. George will become a stronger shepherd because he has built a team around him which can augment his strengths.

Let me take you back to my comment about married singles. Don't find someone with traits opposite of yours, then let him go and do his thing. The only way opposites on a team build a strong ministry is by supplementing each other's efforts. When each of you is working on a common goal by contributing to its completion, you will be fulfilling Paul's prayer that we use the Spirit's gift for the common good (1 Cor. 12:7).

Project for Chapter 4

Myron Rush is the author of the test distributed by Management Training Systems of Colorado Springs, Colorado.

Have each team member take the Temperament Test and score himself according to the directions. Keep in mind that no one temperament is right and the other wrong, and that your personality is not comprised exclusively of one of the four temperaments. You are a composite of the four. No doubt one will be more dominant than the others. Using the traits on this test, make a list as shown on "Your Management Temperament Profile."

When all team members have finished scoring the test, discuss your scores and determine if they agree with the way you perceive each other. Next discuss how you can better augment each other's ministries with your strengths. Dig into your current team's history, so you will have some live illustrations to work with.

The circle with the weaknesses and strengths will give you a good definition of the four temperaments. To help you better understand who these people are, here is a simple characterization of each.

A. Promotional Manager

He generally has the ability to excite or motivate people for short periods of time. He can usually smile when the bottom falls out and can cause a group of discouraged people to get their emotions back in balance. He has a certain level of people-orientation, which makes him want to help them get out of their depression or solve their problem. He likes to be in charge but often doesn't have an actual plan to improve the situation. Although he can encourage people, he lacks the discipline necessary to carry out a plan that another person may suggest. Even if he starts to do so, he will probably not carry through with the project. You will often find him in the middle of a conversation at a social gathering. People enjoy being around him because he is friendly and carefree.

He needs someone else on the team who can design the actual plan to solve the problem. He also needs someone who can conceive of all the small details that make the event run smoothly and who has the discipline to carry out the plan.

B. Concept Manager

Because he has the theoretical or idealistic view of how to solve the group's problems, he falls into the trap of not being able to complete the plan because he is a perfectionist. Perfectionists seldom get the job done because it cannot be done perfectly; and until it can, there is no reason to do it. With his analytical mind he can come up with the solution to the problem, but may not want to do so because most approaches won't work. Consequently, he becomes his own worst critic.

He needs someone to work with him who is willing to try a plan, even if it isn't perfect, and a group of people who still need some maturity or training.

C. Operational Manager

He is the person who conceives of himself as the natural strong leader. He is a strong-willed person. In fact, he is so strong-willed that he will even make a bad decision work. He is positive and practical. He can show the concept manager why his idea will work. Because he is such a strong-willed person you may find him doing the work by himself. This may be because he thinks people don't understand him. The fact that he has poor relational skills may further augment this problem.

He really needs a negotiating manager who can help him get along with the people in his group. Because he is so anxious to get the task accomplished, he may tend to run over people who won't go along with his plan.

D. Negotiating Manager

If you have a conflict in your organization, he can help you solve it. Part of the reason for this is that he will not take sides in an issue. He will stay unemotionally involved when tension is mounting over a critical issue. It's obvious then that he is diplomatic. You may often find him in a detailed task, such as treasurer.

He needs team members who can conceive of plans and ideas to solve organizational problems. Because he tends to be the spectator, he needs someone like an operational manager who can organize and direct the affairs of the organization.

Temperament Test *

Name ______________________________

Rate yourself as to the extent the following characteristics represent you. Rate yourself on each characteristic with 10, most like you, 1, least like you.

A Score ______
200

Outgoing, Sociable	1 2 3 4 5 6 7 8 9 10
Inspires Allegiance	1 2 3 4 5 6 7 8 9 10
Sincere	1 2 3 4 5 6 7 8 9 10
Positive Attitude	1 2 3 4 5 6 7 8 9 10
Responsive to Others	1 2 3 4 5 6 7 8 9 10
Talkative	1 2 3 4 5 6 7 8 9 10
Enthusiastic	1 2 3 4 5 6 7 8 9 10
Seldom Worries	1 2 3 4 5 6 7 8 9 10
Compassionate	1 2 3 4 5 6 7 8 9 10
Generous	1 2 3 4 5 6 7 8 9 10
Undisciplined	1 2 3 4 5 6 7 8 9 10
Easily Influenced	1 2 3 4 5 6 7 8 9 10
Restless	1 2 3 4 5 6 7 8 9 10
Disorganized	1 2 3 4 5 6 7 8 9 10
Undependable	1 2 3 4 5 6 7 8 9 10
Loud	1 2 3 4 5 6 7 8 9 10
Promotes Self	1 2 3 4 5 6 7 8 9 10
Exaggerates	1 2 3 4 5 6 7 8 9 10
Fearful, Insecure	1 2 3 4 5 6 7 8 9 10
Unproductive	1 2 3 4 5 6 7 8 9 10

B Score ______
200

Natural Talent	1 2 3 4 5 6 7 8 9 10
Analytical	1 2 3 4 5 6 7 8 9 10
Perfectionist	1 2 3 4 5 6 7 8 9 10
Conscientious	1 2 3 4 5 6 7 8 9 10
Loyal	1 2 3 4 5 6 7 8 9 10
Aesthetic	1 2 3 4 5 6 7 8 9 10
Idealistic	1 2 3 4 5 6 7 8 9 10
Sensitive	1 2 3 4 5 6 7 8 9 10
Self-sacrificing	1 2 3 4 5 6 7 8 9 10
Self-disciplined	1 2 3 4 5 6 7 8 9 10
Moody	1 2 3 4 5 6 7 8 9 10
Negative	1 2 3 4 5 6 7 8 9 10
Critical	1 2 3 4 5 6 7 8 9 10
Resists Change	1 2 3 4 5 6 7 8 9 10
Self-conscious	1 2 3 4 5 6 7 8 9 10
Unpredictable	1 2 3 4 5 6 7 8 9 10
Revengeful	1 2 3 4 5 6 7 8 9 10
Lacks Self-confidence	1 2 3 4 5 6 7 8 9 10
Unsociable	1 2 3 4 5 6 7 8 9 10
Theoretical	1 2 3 4 5 6 7 8 9 10

C Score ______
200

Determined	1 2 3 4 5 6 7 8 9 10
Independent	1 2 3 4 5 6 7 8 9 10
Productive	1 2 3 4 5 6 7 8 9 10
Decisive	1 2 3 4 5 6 7 8 9 10
Practical	1 2 3 4 5 6 7 8 9 10
Goal Oriented	1 2 3 4 5 6 7 8 9 10
Optimistic	1 2 3 4 5 6 7 8 9 10
Willing To Risk	1 2 3 4 5 6 7 8 9 10
Self-confident	1 2 3 4 5 6 7 8 9 10
Willing To Lead	1 2 3 4 5 6 7 8 9 10
Unsympathetic	1 2 3 4 5 6 7 8 9 10
Inconsiderate	1 2 3 4 5 6 7 8 9 10
Resists Regulations	1 2 3 4 5 6 7 8 9 10
Cruel, Sarcastic	1 2 3 4 5 6 7 8 9 10
Doesn't Give Recognition	1 2 3 4 5 6 7 8 9 10
Self-sufficient	1 2 3 4 5 6 7 8 9 10
Domineering	1 2 3 4 5 6 7 8 9 10
Opinionated	1 2 3 4 5 6 7 8 9 10
Proud	1 2 3 4 5 6 7 8 9 10
Cunning	1 2 3 4 5 6 7 8 9 10

D Score ______
200

Calm, Quiet	1 2 3 4 5 6 7 8 9 10
Easy Going	1 2 3 4 5 6 7 8 9 10
Likeable	1 2 3 4 5 6 7 8 9 10
Diplomatic	1 2 3 4 5 6 7 8 9 10
Efficient, Organized	1 2 3 4 5 6 7 8 9 10
Dependable, Stable	1 2 3 4 5 6 7 8 9 10
Conservative	1 2 3 4 5 6 7 8 9 10
Practical	1 2 3 4 5 6 7 8 9 10
Reluctant Leader	1 2 3 4 5 6 7 8 9 10
Dry Humor	1 2 3 4 5 6 7 8 9 10
Unmotivated	1 2 3 4 5 6 7 8 9 10
Unexcitable	1 2 3 4 5 6 7 8 9 10
Avoids Conflict	1 2 3 4 5 6 7 8 9 10
Spectator	1 2 3 4 5 6 7 8 9 10
Selfish	1 2 3 4 5 6 7 8 9 10
Stingy	1 2 3 4 5 6 7 8 9 10
Stubborn	1 2 3 4 5 6 7 8 9 10
Self-protective	1 2 3 4 5 6 7 8 9 10
Indecisive	1 2 3 4 5 6 7 8 9 10
Fear of Risk	1 2 3 4 5 6 7 8 9 10

*Management Temperament Test used by permission of Myron Rush

Your Management Temperament Profile

Instructions

Review your management temperament test. Record below each temperament trait receiving a score of seven or more. Place an "X" in the score column corresponding with the score of each trait being listed.

Your management temperament profile consists of all of your management temperament traits receiving a score of seven or more regardless of their management temperament classification.

Dominators

Management Temperament Dominators are those traits receiving a score of 7-8. These management temperament traits tend to dominate the other "weaker" traits.

Regulators

Management Temperament Regulators are those traits receiving a score of 9-10. They represent the strongest drive in one's management temperament makeup and provide the greatest input toward how the manager acts or reacts in a given management situation.

	Dominators		Regulators	
MANAGEMENT TEMPERAMENT TRAIT	**7**	**8**	**9**	**10**

Temperaments

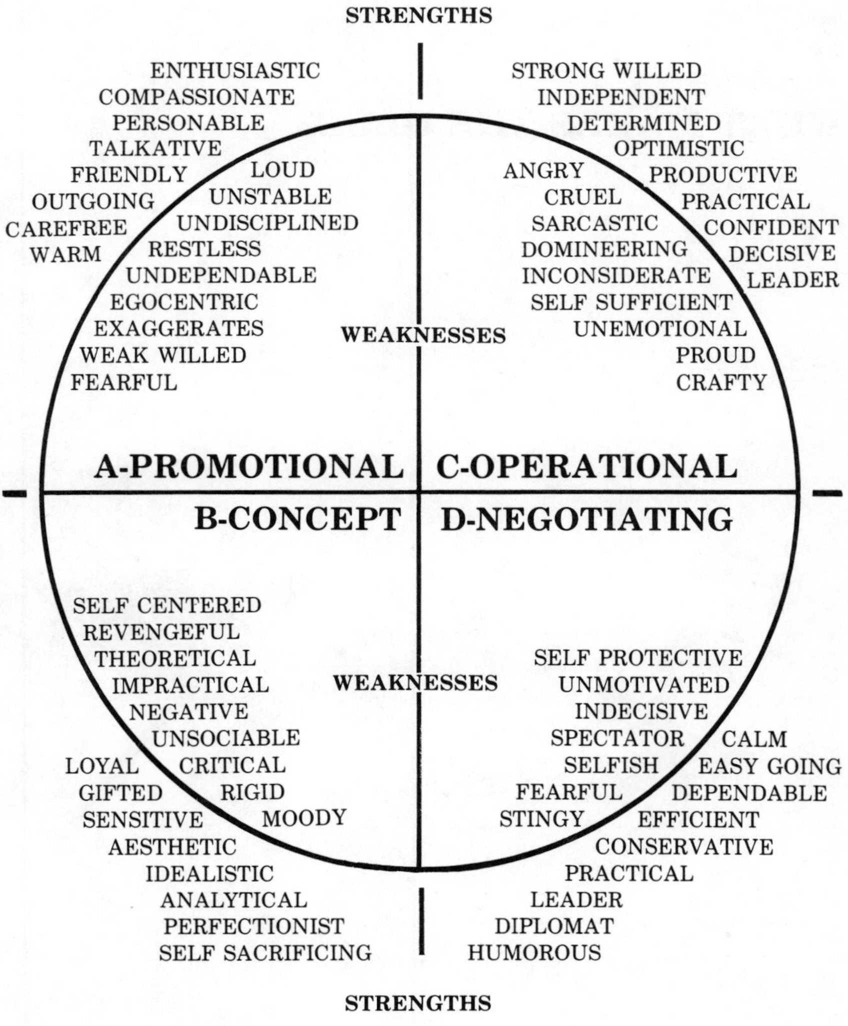
STRENGTHS
ENTHUSIASTIC
COMPASSIONATE
PERSONABLE
TALKATIVE
FRIENDLY
OUTGOING
CAREFREE
WARM
LOUD
UNSTABLE
UNDISCIPLINED
RESTLESS
UNDEPENDABLE
EGOCENTRIC
EXAGGERATES
WEAK WILLED
FEARFUL
STRONG WILLED
INDEPENDENT
DETERMINED
OPTIMISTIC
PRODUCTIVE
PRACTICAL
CONFIDENT
DECISIVE
LEADER
ANGRY
CRUEL
SARCASTIC
DOMINEERING
INCONSIDERATE
SELF SUFFICIENT
UNEMOTIONAL
PROUD
CRAFTY
WEAKNESSES
A-PROMOTIONAL
C-OPERATIONAL
B-CONCEPT
D-NEGOTIATING
SELF CENTERED
REVENGEFUL
THEORETICAL
IMPRACTICAL
NEGATIVE
UNSOCIABLE
CRITICAL
RIGID
MOODY
LOYAL
GIFTED
SENSITIVE
AESTHETIC
IDEALISTIC
ANALYTICAL
PERFECTIONIST
SELF SACRIFICING
WEAKNESSES
SELF PROTECTIVE
UNMOTIVATED
INDECISIVE
SPECTATOR
SELFISH
FEARFUL
STINGY
CALM
EASY GOING
DEPENDABLE
EFFICIENT
CONSERVATIVE
PRACTICAL
LEADER
DIPLOMAT
HUMOROUS
STRENGTHS

Part II: **The Functioning of a Team**

5

WHAT MAKES THE GLUE?

"I want you all to remember that we are a team."

5

WHAT MAKES THE GLUE?

FOR YEARS THE church of Jesus Christ was concerned about the disintegration of the American home in secular society. It's no secret — that forest fire has spread across to the other side of the road, to the church. If a Christian home today is to fend off the vicious enemies of society, it needs strong glue to hold it together internally. The same is true of a church staff. Like a family, it can be the most beautiful experience humans can know, or it can be as horrid as a raging forest fire. No family or church staff can ward off its pending destroyer unless it is committed to make itself all that God intended it to be. Each member will need to draw upon the available power of God's Holy Spirit to express His divine love.

Just as the church is both a theological and a sociological institution, so is its staff. The sociologist would call the staff a social system, which is a term to designate a definable group of persons who are within an orbit of interpersonal relationships. Charles Loomis, an eminent sociologist, says there are nine elements in the social system: belief; sentiment; goal, end, or objective; norm; status-role; rank; power; sanction; and facility.[1]

The sociologist would say that when these elements are functioning at their best, a social system has achieved its potential. I have studied the theories by other sociologists, such as Malcomb Knowles, Darwin Cartwright, and Alvin Zander. Each one gives us a certain insight into a social system. But because of their limited perspective, they cannot apply the theological or spiritual elements to the social system of a church staff and to the body of Christ. It is my opinion, therefore, that the church staff must be viewed in an additional way. We can apply the social system principles, but that only gets us so far.

The fact that the staff not only has its own system to be concerned with, but also has a unique relationship with the congregation, brings a whole different set of principles to play upon that system. Each church varies, too, in its organizational structure.

Try to grasp the complexity of that social system by looking at just one example. Trinity Church has six staff members. Each one had a diverse church experience in his developmental years. They each had a unique educational background and were influenced by their prior various service experiences. The relationships with those other staff people, their stages in their spiritual pilgrimage, their church organizational structure, the Holy Spirit's influence upon them, the way authority was viewed and used, the type of community, the history of that congregation, and the era of American culture all influenced the way they came to that team. The roles, spiritual depth, relationship, and expectations of not only the laity they work with, but also the whole congregation, must be considered. Every time the team sits down to a staff meeting to discuss anything and make a decision, they are looking at the issue through this whole grid of influences.

That's a small peek at a church staff social system. I choose to call it a social-theological (spiritual) system because of the interplay of these two dynamic sets of forces. Each one has a great influence upon the formation and functioning of the system.

In the rest of this chapter we will look at the elements that make up an ideal staff system. These are the ideals you will need to work on, or the glue that will hold the team together. I'm going to use cultural word pictures that will define this ideal team and which will also show how the team can best function. Illustrations will show ways you can develop that godly unity and commitment to each other to keep staff infection from destroying what God most desires for your team. The word pictures have similar elements which make them look somewhat alike, but each has a salient characteristic which will give us another window into a strong staff system.

The Family's Feelings of Roots

When my wife and I graduated from high school, we both moved away from our families. For a few years we lived in nearby states, but for twenty-five years now we have been separated from our roots by thousands of miles. Even though we occasionally see family members over the years, we have a hard time relating to our families. We have lost the sense of "we-ness." In spite of that, we continue to feel the pull of wanting to go home. There we can count on being accepted and respected. We can sympathize with Israel when they were in Egypt. They belonged to a different land; their souls would never be at rest, until they could be in their homeland. The T.V. story of Halley's *Roots* touched a vital nerve in the heart of many human beings, especially those who have been separated from their roots. We could all identify with that strong need for a sense of belonging. Nothing in our human experience better describes that feeling than being a member of a healthy family. No wonder so many Scripture writers liken our becoming Christians to our joining the family of God. This appeals to us. In the body of Christ we can sing with deep feeling, "I'm so glad I'm a part of the family of God."

An ideal church staff needs this basic element of family as their foundation for a good social-theological system. It takes more than the knowledge that they all belong to Christ and to the local church. It takes family-like attitudes and activities to build a good social-theological system. Each member must be taken seriously. No member of the family will allow another family member to be seen in public with egg on his face. When sin creeps in, the others forgive and aid in healing. They will truly "bear one another's burdens." When a new, young, energetic staff member falls on his face, a healthy family will pick him up and help him walk.

No place on earth is there more intimacy and confidentiality practiced than at home. There we may argue among ourselves, but we will give our last ounce of energy dying for a family member. We need to be like picture-carrying grandparents who are always bragging about their family. They brag in public and in private. Like grandparents, we need to have a harder time acknowledging our family members' faults, and a quicker tendency to brag about any good traits that we can find. This doesn't mean that there isn't any conflict, but a strong family knows how to iron out differences so that everyone is still accepted and still wants to be with the family. The members will stay committed to each other until time heals their wounds. For this to happen, there must be dialogue, a lot of time spent together, and a deep commitment to everyone else's wellbeing.

A strong percentage of the children who are adopted into a godly, loving family seem to overcome many of the handicaps they brought with them. Wouldn't it be great if each staff member who was adopted as a part of your team felt as if he had been grafted into your roots?

When the staff has this kind of "we-ness," the congregation sees it and feels it. They soon learn how to practice body life as well. What a difference this will make in staff meetings, in church services, and in committee meetings. May God make you a great family!

The Corporate Drive for Productivity

The phrase, "the bottom line," was born in the heart of American industry. We are known for it the world over. Champagne corks are popped when the boss announces that this year's profit exceeded last year's. The manager has a word of praise for every department because he knows that everybody, from the stock room clerk and secretaries to the salesmen out on the road, made it happen. It took the skill of the draftsman and the faithfulness of the assembly-line worker to make it possible. Each department recognizes this, even though their functions are unique. They are all working diligently, trying to accomplish the same goal.

That's what Paul had in mind in 1 Corinthians 12:12-13 (NIV). "The body is a unit, though it is made up of many parts; and though all its parts are many, they form one body. So it is with Christ. For we were all baptized by one Spirit into one body — whether Jews or Greeks, slave or free — and we were all given the one Spirit to drink."

A team member who is concerned about modeling the unity of the microcosm is concerned about the development of the whole body, not just his or her special segment of the program. A youth minister rejoices just as much over the growth of the choir as he does over the qualitative and quantitative growth of the youth department. In fact, he's the one who ought to stand before the congregation once in awhile and do the choir recruiting.

The macho youth pastor with his strong task orientation and objective viewpoint, after a three-hour staff meeting in the midst of a hectic day, sits across the room from the minister of music, who has a musician's subjective temperament. They are struggling through a decision about what to do with Jim. He's supposed to go on the youth choir tour, which will be departing tomorrow. Jim has just been caught in a lie about fulfilling the qualifications to go on the tour. The musician needs Jim's voice so much that he is willing to overlook the sin, because Jim has asked for forgiveness and has received it. The youth pastor thinks he ought to stay at home to emphasize and reinforce the discipline. What's the bottom line? Now it is not anybody's program that counts. It is the growth of the body of Christ. A productive team acknowledges this as the bottom line.

In a secular corporation the bottom line isn't always on the credit side. Sometimes it is the result of one department that hasn't done its job well. It lacked the creativity and the drive necessary to make the production quota. The whole corporation team will not receive bonuses this year. It's so easy to judge, criticize, and feel hostility. This is where the social system needs to become a social-spiritual system. A sense of love and acceptance is necessary.

The Peace Church has five staff members. This particular group has labored together in love for over five years. Some have been there longer, with Pastor Smith having preached for fourteen years. He just had his sixty-third birthday. His preaching is far less effective than it was even three years ago. Consequently, the attendance is falling off radically. He doesn't want to retire for some years, but many in the congregation wish he would take early retirement. When the young associate preaches, people are enthusiastic. Pastor Smith has few staff meetings now, which tends to build up even more tension among the staff, who are very much aware of the congregation's dissatisfaction. Now what's the bottom line? Is this a social system or a social-theological system?

Cartwright says that a social system becomes effective and functions harmoniously "to the degree to which the activities of different members are coordinated in a manner required by the group tasks." The humanistic viewpoint reflected in the social system would say that the Peace Church team can no longer function as an effective system. Even spiritually a lot of things are against it. Because those spiritual beings haven't all developed to the level of maturity necessary to make a success of the situation, harmony and effectiveness are tenuous. The younger men on the team find their whole future ministry in jeopardy. They may see their lack of success now as a hindrance to their chances for a greater challenge in the years to come. But what's the standard of measurement? Isn't the mature way in which they make this system work really the greatest step of maturity they could ever know?

If this is a genuine spiritually-based system, then they need to work out the tensions. It could mean that Pastor Smith should take an earlier retirement, or restructure the team's operation. The thing that will make the difference is how the situation is handled. The team must have the freedom, love, and transparency to deal with the problems. It will take giving on the part of everyone. They will need to prove that the spiritual way is truly the greater way to deal with ineffectiveness. The true way is not to ignore it, but to handle it with tenderness and wisdom.

The Athlete's Commonly Owned Goal

There may be some question about the goals of the teams I've mentioned thus far, but there should never be a question about the goal of an athletic team. The members of an athletic team know the agony of defeat and the thrill of winning. They know what it means to play or work in adverse circumstances. They know what it means to be praised and to be hissed off the field. They know what one person's carelessness can mean to the whole team, even to their own history. You can count on one thing. They readily recognize their common goal — win! win! win! They quickly identify Paul cheering from the bench, "Press towards the prize of the high calling of God in Christ Jesus." A team member doesn't want to let others down, or to be the one who strikes out with the bases loaded in the last inning when the team is trailing by three runs.

One of the most inspiring athletic scenes I've ever seen occurred in the final NCAA Basketball Tournament in 1982. Georgetown and North Carolina weren't more than three points apart the whole contest. Georgetown had its last chance, with eleven seconds left to win its first national championship. Then the only serious mistake of the whole game occurred. In the tenseness of the moment, a Georgetown guard threw the ball to one of the "tar heels" and he won the game for them. That would be enough to break any coach's heart, but with a look of love on his face, the Georgetown coach walked out onto the court and hugged the guard, who was utterly crushed. The coach said, "You threw the ball right all the other times. If it hadn't been for your good playing, we wouldn't have made it this far. Don't feel bad; you are forgiven." I wish I could see that spirit displayed more often on church staffs.

Early in my preaching experience I was sure I had laid the biggest rotten egg ever laid in history. I could hardly wait until I was finished so I could run home. And sure enough, that is just what I did. As soon as the "Amen" was expressed, I disappeared out the back door and went directly home. Dr. Herbert Anderson, my fellow staff member, greeted me with a loving spirit an hour later and wanted to know where I had gone. His love and acceptance of me, and his words, "There wasn't anything wrong," allowed me to give it another try very soon.

A social-spiritual system, like an athletic team, plays together to win. The other team members pay the price of giving that extra ounce of energy to make up for the one whose soul hurts and who is having some great struggles. The team is determined to win. In their team meetings and review huddles, they continually think through new strategies because they are determined to see the church of Jesus Christ go forward like a mighty army.

The Theologian's Binding Issues

It may seem strange to you if I choose theologians to represent a word picture of a social-theological system. Theologians tend to be isolators who pick apart their colleague's viewpoint. Like the other social word pictures, one unique feature makes them stand out as a great picture of a social-spiritual team.

They have taken all the time necessary to study, have sifted through the various positions, have checked every possible authority, and are now ready to die for the absolutes they have settled upon. I see this especially in a new denomination, or even a new theological institution. Theologians were drawn together by their studied convictions. They will give up their friends, the buildings they own, or even their retirement funds. Many have or would be willing to die for their convictions, based on God's Word. A great team is held together by their biblical convictions.

When you apply this picture to a social-spiritual system, it spreads out a little to include philosophical principles. Certain priorities and strategies guide their expenditure of energy and finances. Time and experience have proven to them that, for their church at this time, given this team, there is one way to do things. Ask anyone on a strong team the same question and he will have, like the others, one basic answer. It's been studied, discussed from every possible angle, and for them, this is the way to go. They will also tell you that there are certain issues which are not important at all. That's part of their conviction system.

Richard is the associate pastor of the Church in the Pines. His sister has asked him to perform her wedding. She is not a member of the church. Even though she professes Christ as Lord and Savior, she is marrying an avowed non-Christian. The Church in the Pines staff has studied long and hard on this issue and has come to the conclusion that their staff will not participate in such a wedding. A social-theological system stands together because each team member is committed to the team's theological-philosophical set of convictions. They all know what they stand for and why, and they will not make an exception without a unanimous decision.

The chapter in Part I about writing a church and staff philosophy statement should make more sense now than before. When you face an issue with no studied conviction, before you can give an answer to the inquirer, you must get the team together and make a decision. That is a time-consuming task, but how safe and wholesome to be able to say that, after much study and prayer, this is the decision of the team. Many a person has stepped out by himself on a vital issue and isolated himself from the team or other church members just because the team had not come to a decision in the matter. May your team keep singing their theme song, "We Are One in the Bond of Love," or "Bless Be the Tie That Binds Our Hearts in Christian Love."

The Marriage's Common Commitment

A married couple is part of the larger family. Many things are similar between a marriage and a family, but there are differences, too. The Lord has instructed families to separate, but He has commanded marriages never to separate. Children don't choose their parents and siblings, but marriage partners have the thrill of choosing each other. God says that families should not uncover each other, but marriages thrive on it.

Alan Lay McGinnis in *Friendship Factor* reminds us that marriages ought to be built on commitment to each other, rather than merely on love.[2] The great number of American marriage breakups reveal a lack of this one critical factor, commitment. Few people know what that means anymore. Perhaps this is the reason the social-theological system reflects the same tendency toward breakup as secular marriages. A staff needs commitment as part of the glue that makes it a strong system. Congregations tend to be slow to make commitments on building programs and other long term programs, because they have this terrible feeling that their leaders won't be around to see the project through to completion.

Commitment in no way means continual days of bliss and happiness. It means, "I'm committed to you even when sickness and irritation set in. I'm committed to you even when you develop distasteful habits." With commitment, you can build a strong staff, which in turn builds a strong congregation. Isn't that what the patriarchs had to learn in their walk with the Lord — unswerving commitment even when they couldn't see through the dark clouds of despair? Our people will learn about commitment to the Lord when they see the staff committed to each other even through adversity.

A pastor moved from California to a church in one of the Plains states. He soon gathered his staff, adding two highly gifted men. They questioned the pastor in the recruiting procedure about his intended tenure. "I'll be here for years," he quickly replied. Everything was going along smoothly when the pastor felt restless. "This congregation isn't all that I would like to see," he reasoned to his conscience. Soon he moved away, and left two deeply disappointed staff men. Their tenure was in jeopardy as the next pastor came to his new charge. What values did the congregation learn from that? What a poor lesson those two seminarians learned from this supposedly seasoned pastor!

The Scientist's Studied Insight

Pastor Jerry and Youth Pastor Steve were with their youth on a snow retreat. They both suffered from the fatigue of short nights and too much exercise. Jerry was unhappy with the way Steve was handling the discipline of the couples late in the evening. He snapped at Steve out of his tired frustration. Steve was so shocked he turned and walked away. Now Jerry was even more angry. The next Tuesday, Jerry approached Steve in the quietness of his office. A healthy, forgiving attitude followed. They both learned a new respect for each other.

Two weeks later they saw the same kind of thing happen at the church board meeting. Jerry looked at Steve and, with a sense of deep understanding, gave him a wink. That wink told a five-day story of anger, acceptance, and love that only a studied, scientific-type team member could understand. They had both looked deeply into the test tube of life and learned about its makeup.

A team of scientists spent five years in a laboratory seeking to unfold the mystery of a common disease. They kept looking at the same cells and discussing what they saw. They soon built a whole new language for their system of research. When they looked into those X-rays and test tubes, they both saw the same thing. If you were to walk into their lab and listen to them, you might not have the foggiest idea about what they were speaking.

A social-theological system has built a studied perception because they are always talking about the dynamics of what's going on in the life of their congregation. Larry Richards calls this the "lived moment."[3] It's the ability to discuss in depth an actual event as it is occurring. Over the years a depth of understanding is accumulated about most of the events that transpire in a team's ministry together. It becomes increasingly easier to communicate and reach a decision about the next move because of the team's studied and dialogued experiences. Marriage partners, after years of marriage, have logged many "lived moments" which greatly aid their communication skills. When one of the children makes a comment, a simple wink of the eye flashes from one mind to the other, a buildup of years of "lived moments."

You ought to be able to understand now why there are similarities between a secular social system and a theological system. The Spirit of God truly gives us capabilities far beyond a group of people who work together in a corporate headquarters, or who play on a professional athletic team together. My deep prayer for your team is that it can experience the deep meaning of a social-theological (spiritual) system.

Project for Chapter 5

A. Measuring Rods

Dody Donnelly in his book called *Team* has a section entitled, "Common Experience: Measuring Rods for Membership." His model of a social system has been an inspiration to me to build my social-theological system. Note under each of the six points a further explanation of its meaning.

Ask each member of the team to mark on a one-to-six continuum where they perceive your staff to be with number 1 being very weak and number 6 very strong. When each is finished, build a composite which will give you a reading on where your staff is strong and weak. In the discussion that follows, make some decisions about how you can actually see growth in those weak areas.

Common Experience: Measuring Rods for Membership[4]

For the team to work well together some *shared elements* help measure the growing we hope for; they help us experience what a real team might be, and we experience them together.

1. *Shared Sense of Belonging*: We might ask to test for these:
   Do members feel they belong to the group?
   Do they feel really respected, welcome?
   Are they really part of the planning, the work, the deciding, the responsibility?
   Are their ideas listened to, accepted?
   Are they taken seriously, especially if they are women?
   Do members feel that belonging to this team is so satisfying that it really makes it worth the effort to belong?
2. *Shared Achievement*
   Is the team aware that, to function at their best, belonging, respect for differences, expression of feeling, open decision-making — all shared in co-responsibility — are essential for successful working together?
   Can members see their individual achievement contributing to the mosaic of the team's work, so to the *teamwork*?
   Gradually, can "success" fade as a goal or criterion for valuing one another, and "serving-and-loving" become *achievement* for this team?
3. *See-Level as Basis of Human Difference*
   Do members reflect long and hard before they see another's reaction as dislike or aversion?

Rather, can they gain perspective through interpreting most reactions as coming from the other's culture, education, experience, environmental pressures, disappointed expectations? (See-Level got stomped on?)

Can each develop the habit of fostering the others' See-Levels with his unique gifts, skills, experiences making for team-richness and the Spirit's power released?

Do members deepen their acceptance of their *own* See-Levels as producing their attitudes and sometimes unaccountable behavior? It's better than counting to ten!

4. *Shared Accountability*

How much real responsibility do members feel to the team life and work?

What mechanisms keep them honest by sharing of "goofs" and "glows"?

Has the team designed a way to let people get these both out on the carpet?

Can they share them in prayer as well, keeping our "trying-to-be-honest" in full view of the Spirit's power to help us be?

Who is accountable to whom, and do they both know and accept that?

5. *Shared Ideas, Insights, and Feelings*

Can the team members express to each other through their structure, as well as informally, what they think, their learning from experiences, their deepest feelings? Disappointment, despair, frustration, joy, exultation?

How to work out ways so that these feelings can be channeled, not discouraged, evoked rather than suppressed?

What provision is there in the weekly staff meeting for such expression?

How much do the members know about communications skills, methods, training?

6. *Shared Theological Reflection and Prayer*

Can the team take time periodically for serious study, discussing (with a resource person, perhaps) the *theory* of the kind of serving they're trying to do?

How does the team facilitate such digging into practice to find its basis in the teaching of Jesus?

Most importantly, will the team set up special periods for communal prayer, not satisfied with individual prayer, though building on it?

Can responsibility for such prayer move around the group, respecting the contributions of each?

Does the team see prayer as a help in making decisions, another way to "work through" a problem, an idea, a decision? Not only thinking it through, but laying themselves open to the Spirit's teaching them in prayer, and listening?

B. Group Dynamics

Once you have worked through your composite of Donnelly's social system model, you may find it helpful to examine Cartwright and Zander's "Group Dynamics" system. They have listed the six elements which are most detrimental to group effectiveness. Note the similarity between Donnelly's system and Cartwright and Zander's system. The first is positive and the second, negative. This study should prove a great help in clearing up the weaknesses discovered in Project A.

Most Detrimental Aspects of Group Effectiveness [5]

1. The extent to which a clear goal is present.
2. The degree to which the group goal mobilizes energies of group members behind group activities.
3. The degree to which there is conflict among members concerning which one of several possible goals should control the activities of the group.
4. The degree to which there is conflict among members concerning means that the group should employ in reaching its goals.
5. The degree to which the activities of different members are coordinated in a manner required by the group's tasks.
6. The availability to the group of needed resources, whether they be economic, material, legal, intellectual, or other.

Part II: **The Functioning of a Team**

6

DESCRIBING YOUR MISSION

"Somehow I don't think the new youth pastor is fitting in."

6

DESCRIBING YOUR MISSION

THIS CHAPTER and the next are like Siamese twins; they can't be separated. They sound very much alike. This chapter concerns developing and maintaining job descriptions, and the next chapter deals with role clarification. Usually the development of a job description precedes a role clarification exercise, and that is why this chapter comes first. (In some church situations their order may be reversed.) These chapters are also similar in that they are both ongoing experiences for a healthy church.

Complete the first draft of a job description before a new staff person is hired. About six months to a year after the person has been on the job, review the job description. By that time the new team member will better understand his task, his team, and the congregation. His team will better understand who he is, what his gifts and temperament are, and what contribution he can best make. At that time you can solidify a more permanent job description, but even that should go through continuous reviews.

It's likely that the whole team will want to go through a role clarification exercise before you complete that more permanent job description for your new staff person. It is likely that everyone's job description may be changed at that time. In the next chapter we'll discover how the team members' jobs intertwine, but for now let's concentrate on the job description.

Job descriptions are not guarantees that your team will be a more solidified and prosperous team, but they can and have saved churches from crises. I've seen many beautiful, growing, and productive teams who never wrote a job description for anyone at their church, but I've also seen church splits ruin the cause of Christ in a community for years, because they had no description. A recent survey in the Southern Baptist movement indicated that forty-two percent of the staff people do not have job descriptions. Even though job descriptions aren't cure-alls, let's consider their advantages.

Advantages of Job Descriptions

1. Job descriptions greatly *aid the church in narrowing down the field of prospective candidates for a new staff position.* If you don't specify details about how narrow or how all-encompassing the new ministry is to be, you may find yourself corresponding with three times as many candidates as you need.
2. A job description will *aid the new worker in knowing what he's to do,* and will guard him from a diversified role expectation by the congregation. When Jerry walked into the sanctuary on his first Sunday at Liberty Church, everyone was excited because they had a new Christian education director. One family knew he could help them reach their wayward son. Someone else was sure the Sunday school classes would now be better taught. One couple, who were committed to their faltering denominational club program, thought the club would finally get the attention it deserved. Six teachers were ready to quit because of burnout; they were sure that their new minister could readily solve their problems. The Christian Education Board knew that the sagging Sunday school attendance would soon be turned around.

   Everyone in the congregation had a different expectation for Jerry, who within a year would be royally roasted by the majority of the congregation. The members were never told what he was to do, and neither was Jerry. Thus he went about doing what he enjoyed doing most. He loved to study and counsel, and that all seemed to fit into his job description. What made it worse was that the senior pastor said, "I'll stand back and let you direct the program as you see fit, because I don't know anything about C.E." The conclusion of this case can be duplicated many times — a bitter congregation, a turned-off servant of God, and a church reluctant to hire anyone else to build a strong church educational program.
3. Job descriptions will *clarify relationships between jobs,* thus avoiding overlaps and gaps. You'll notice I state often, in this book, how complex things become when a new staff member is added. The same tasks are there to be done as before, but now who's going to do what and when? A church isn't a factory where you switch a person to another machine when you have someone else to care for the task he did on the assembly line.

While one person may have overseen the whole ministry of the church before a second staff person was added, now he may feel relieved because the new staff member can take up half the ministry. The trouble is that neither half will be picked up totally, because the whole was never described in the first place. Without a thorough study of your philosophy and scope of ministry, some major task may be ignored. The likelihood of this is greatly multiplied when your leaders don't take the time and energy to think through the total scope of your church's task, and when they don't write job descriptions.

4. A job description provides *the first step in actual job appraisal.* If no one has written a job description, the pastor, personnel committee, and the congregation will not have a valid standard by which to judge the new worker's effectiveness. You dare not evaluate anyone's labor without a standard of evaluation.
5. Job descriptions *spell out duties, responsibilities, and limits of authority* in a particular position. Even though every possible situation cannot be written out showing where authority needs to be displayed, some guidelines must be provided for doing so. Here is where role clarification exercises can be helpful. More staff conflict arises here perhaps than any other place. To whom and under what circumstances is a person to be accountable is one of the major ingredients to be clarified.
6. Job descriptions *serve as a basis for establishing performance* as the team members relate to organizational goals and philosophy. In the church, there are a thousand ways to do any one task. Thus the church must ask, in light of our church's structure, philosophy, and current goals, what are we expecting from this new staff member? A good job description will soon blend a new worker into the team's philosophy of ministry.

   First Church is committed to evangelism and discipleship. The Church's philosophy statement clarifies that quite succinctly. A good job description will clarify how the new children's worker will accomplish the church's goals in that area.
7. Job descriptions *build status, respect, and motivation* in the minister. I've left this until last because I feel this is the least important, but it is certainly a worthwhile benefit. A good self-image is certainly going to facilitate a team

member's effectiveness. A job description, I believe, keeps one from just being another generalist. Instead it says what he is going to do, and can do, a special task. "I'm more than a flunky. I'm a specialist with skills, gifts, and now a sense of authority."

Job Description Ingredients

You read an ad in the automobile section of your local newspaper. What a deal! You can hardly believe the price for such a car. That is, until you discover that the price includes only the bare essentials. When you finally put the check in the dealer's hand, the car is twice the price.

Cars in many ways are like job descriptions. They both provide basic transportation to get you to your destination, but you can add a hundred things to the simple, basic format which may make them far more serviceable. At the end of this chapter you will find a helpful tool to design your own machine. You can add all the extras you feel are necessary to get you there.

The basic format of a job description should include the following items stated in some simple form.

1. *Bibliographic data* (written for a resident person, not on one designed for a job opening) — This would include job title, person's name, date, and when the job description should be updated.
2. *Ministry purpose* — When a person is engaged in this ministry, he will seek to accomplish the goals listed.
3. *Ministry responsibilities* — Here list the various segments of the ministry or program.
4. *Working relationships* — This would state the one to whom and for whom the person is accountable.
5. *Opportunities* — Include extracurricular activities, such as seminars, conventions, and other ongoing educational experiences.
6. *Qualifications* (To be included for recruiting purposes) — This would include academic, spiritual, ministry skills, and personality or temperament traits.
7. *Financial arrangements* — Show first the *salary* benefits, which would include insurance and vacation. Second, include *business expenses*, such as car and entertainment fees. A new job description should also include moving and settlement allowances.
8. *The organizational chart* — Include in a job description a

pictorial of the groupings of work, people, and superior/subordinate relationships, for all the people involved in the organization. In order to understand your role in relation to your team member's, you will also need to see everyone's relationship to the boards, committees, and groups.

It's easy to see how a fellow-worker will be offended if you bypass him in the flow of authority. Yes, you may hurt his feelings in some instances, but it's more important that you keep everyone informed about what's going on. If the issue at hand is vital to the success of your teams's ministry, then you dare not bypass the ones involved. A well-drawn organizational chart will help to clarify many other aspects of a job description. (See Project A at the end of the chapter for an illustration and instructions for drawing your own.)

Overcoming Dangers of Job Descriptions

Job descriptions do not define ministries, because ministries cut across the whole of the life of the congregation. They tend to deal exclusively with institutional and organizational terms. Because job descriptions are used as evaluation tools, they tend to set the perimeters of ministry along secular lines rather than spiritual lines. In spite of this and other shortcomings, certain guidelines will help you overcome these pitfalls.

1. *The senior pastor should take the lead* or initiative in writing his own job description first. This will be especially important if the church is going to hire its first additional staff person. There is a great deal of inequity in asking a second staff person to function under a job description when the senior pastor has no ministry guidelines or evaluation tool.
2. *Never ask a group to write a job description.* Groups don't think conceptually and their discussion of a job description will degenerate to mere duties rather than objectives. Word order will become more important than conceptualization. They will certainly want to evaluate and ratify a job description, but it is wise to have it designed by the person to whom the staff member will report. A staff person should be concerned with the job description only one level below him. He should not be concerned with those which are any more than one level above him. Before the governing group

evaluates the form, it should be discussed with the person who will be guided by it.

3. *Job descriptions need to be kept up-to-date.* It should be reviewed and reworked at least once a year. It is not to be filed away as an official document of the church; it is a working guideline for an active ministry. It would be unwise to hand down a formerly used job description to a person filling a vacancy.

   When a job description is not kept up-to-date, it can be a strong negative factor. For instance, someone in the congregation might use an antiquated job description, which he considers to be a legal document, as a means of destroying someone he wants to see fired. Another person may get you to do something he himself is supposed to do because it is still listed on your job description. The problem is that this particular task was assigned to someone else three years ago.

   As a person matures and becomes more skilled through experience, and desires to reach out to new challenges, his job description should be changed accordingly. If it isn't, he may find the job losing its appeal and he may look for greener pastures in another church.

4. *Each job description should be personally tailored* by the individuals involved — never should descriptions be mass produced. Consequently, I would be against using documents found in manuals or denominational handbooks. These might be studied as models. Their ideas, phrases, and topics could be a helpful guide in designing your own personally created instrument.

5. *Job descriptions should be looked upon as tools*, and not as documents. A document is an officially binding instrument that rules a person's activities. A tool is more of a general guideline for the work one expects to do. It should be designed to solve specific problems and reach certain objectives. A phrase such as "He shall train the leaders for all of the church's educational ministries," suggests that he will see that they are trained. It doesn't mean that he will do all the training himself. If a job description is looked upon as a document, it is generally considered to be in force immediately upon its acceptance. If it is looked upon as a tool, it takes time for its user to learn to work under its supervision. He should become more proficient at fulfilling its various tasks as the months

roll by. The tool should be carried around in a briefcase or kept in a top drawer and not stored in a vault. It should be dog-eared, coffee stained, and bear frequent pencil marks and question marks as the person actually performs the job and anticipates improvement of his function for the future.

This also says something about the way it should be worded. Use the kind of nouns and verbs that guide a person in a working process, rather than arbitrary and confining words.

6. *Share it with the congregation.* Because each person in the congregation has his or her own unique expectation for each new team member, it's critical that the entire congregation have in their hands a copy of that job description as it is finalized. It is important to notify the congregation about each change so the members will not continue to evaluate their staff members by the old job descriptions.

Now that we've looked at the strengths and weaknesses of a job description, the next chapter will show how they can be strengthened even more through role clarification.

Project for Chapter 6

A. Organizational Chart

Chart these staff people on Organizational Charts as you would anticipate their relationships. Follow the guidelines given on the model.

People on Staff

1. Pastor
   Business Manager
   Youth Pastor
   Christian Education Director
   Children's Director
   Music Director
   Associate of Evangelism and Discipleship
   3 Secretaries (one pastor's secretary)
   Include relationship to these:
   Board of Elders
   Congregation
2. Pastor
   Youth Director
   Children's Director
   2 Secretaries—1 full-time—1 part-time
   Music Director
3. Pastor
   Associate Pastor of Christian Education
   Visitation Pastor
   Church Secretary

B. Developing a Job Description

It is suggested that the following outline be used by the pastor and personnel committee to develop a job description before a prospective staff member is contacted. It may then serve as a guide for the interview and subsequent employment of the staff person. And since changing congregational needs require changing responsibilities, an annual review will be beneficial.

Evaluate your job description in light of the following work sheet. What items should you include or delete?

Job Description for Staff Members

Responsibilities

1. What will be the official title of this staff person?
____
2. What are the primary responsibilities of the staff person?
   a. ______________________________
   b. ______________________________
   c. ______________________________
   d. ______________________________
3. To whom is this staff person responsible?
____
4. What responsibility and authority will this person have, and what budget procedures will be followed?

	RESPONSIBILITY	AUTHORITY
a. Sunday School		
b. Church choirs		
c. Visitation		
d. Public worship services		
e. Public relations and publicity		
f. Week-day clubs		
g. Children's churches		
h. Church nursery		
i. Leadership enlistment		
j. Leadership training		
k. Church business administration		
l. Local church camps		
m. District camps		
n. Vacation Bible School		
o. ______________		
p. ______________		

Opportunities

1. What opportunities will the staff person have to accept invitations and assignments beyond the local church?
   a. State ________________________________
   b. Area ________________________________
   c. Inter-denominational and civic ________________
2. What opportunities will the staff person have to increase his proficiency in his work?
   a. Attendance at local and area functions __________
   b. Attendance at regional and denominational conferences
   ____
   c. Additional class (school) work ________________
3. How will the decisions be made concerning 1 and 2 above, and who will make them?
   ____

Working Relationships

What will be the working relationship with each of the following?

1. Pastor ________________________________
2. Other staff members ________________________
3. Church secretary __________________________
   a. What assistance will be available? __________
4. Custodian ______________________________
5. Official boards
   a. Church board: Attend _____ Report _____ Other _____
   b. Church school board or educational committee:
   Attend ________ Report ________ Other ________
   c. Other boards or committees: ________________
6. Organizational leaders
   a. Sunday school superintendent ________________
   b. Church school board chairman ________________
   c. Other ________________________________
7. Church treasurer __________________________

What will be the normal expectation regarding schedule?

Week-day hours ____________________________
Saturday hours ____________________________
Sunday hours _____________________________
What day off? ____________________________

Is a staff meeting scheduled weekly _____ What day? _____
What office provisions will be made? Room ____ Phone ____

Financial Arrangements

1. Salary ____________
2. Length of vacation ____________
3. Conference and convention expense ____________
4. Housing allowance ____________
5. Utilities ____________
6. Social Security ____________
7. Group Hospitalization ____________
8. Car expense ____________
9. Moving expense ____________
10. Other ____________

In addition to the job description, the following items may be reviewed with the prospective staff member.

1. Has the church had a person in this assignment before? __
   a. Was it a satisfactory experience? ____________
   b. How long did the person serve? ____________
2. Has the pastor had previous experience with a multiple staff?
   a. Was it satisfactory? ____________
   b. How long did the last person serve? ____________
3. What is the expectation of the pastor and the church board relative to the length of time the staff person may serve, assuming he proves a valuable addition to the staff? ____

   ____
4. Will the church be able to provide the agreed compensation without severe strain? ____________

   ____
5. Is there general harmony concerning the employment of a person for this assignment? ____________

   ____

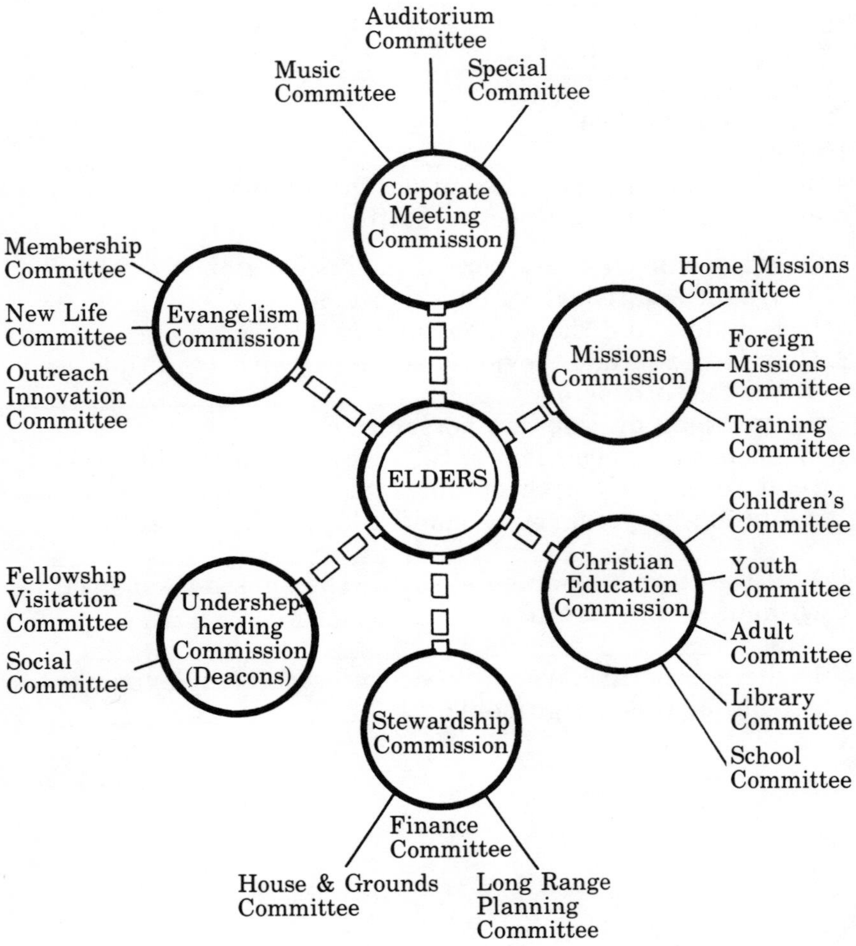
Auditorium Committee
Music Committee
Special Committee
Corporate Meeting Commission
Membership Committee
New Life Committee
Outreach Innovation Committee
Evangelism Commission
Home Missions Committee
Foreign Missions Committee
Training Committee
Missions Commission
ELDERS
Children's Committee
Youth Committee
Adult Committee
Library Committee
School Committee
Christian Education Commission
Fellowship Visitation Committee
Social Committee
Undershep-herding Commission (Deacons)
Stewardship Commission
Finance Committee
House & Grounds Committee
Long Range Planning Committee

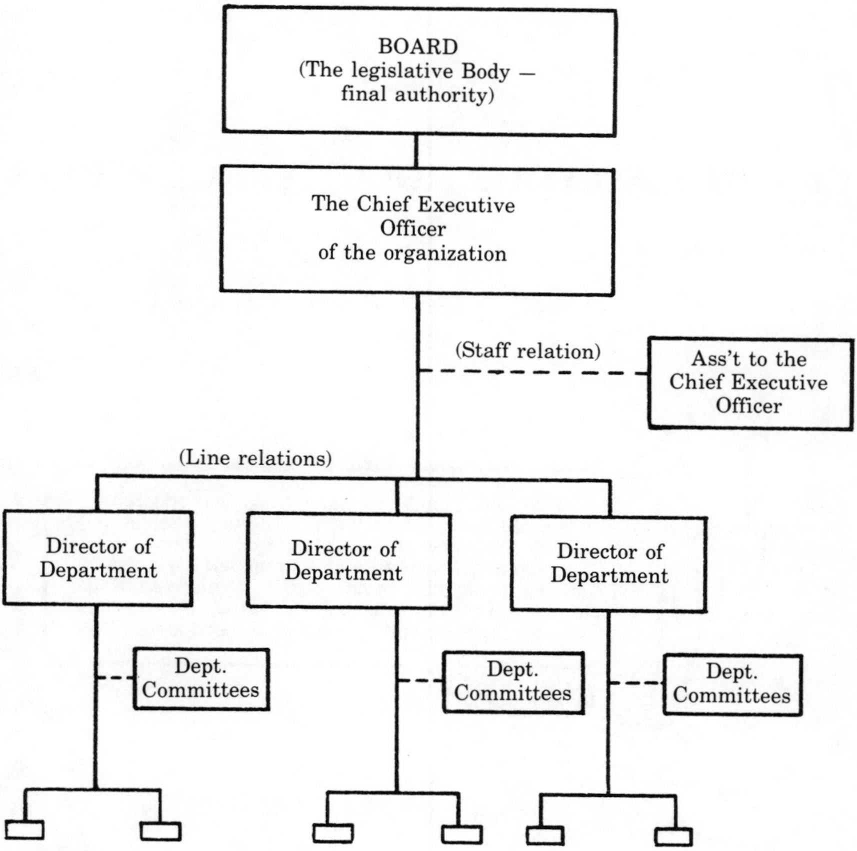

— Solid line indicates authority-accountability relation.
---- Broken line indicates staff relationship — assistant, advisory.

Part II: **The Functioning of a Team**

7

CLARIFYING YOUR ROLE EXPECTATIONS

"Your task, Bob, is to teach 45 spoiled children in Sunday School, lead the Youth group, the senior citizens morning Bible Study, direct the choir, over-see evangelism, serve as role model, counsellor, church picnic director and janitor. If you need assis-tance, you may look for support in the congregation. This tape will self-destruct in 30 seconds. . ."

7

CLARIFYING YOUR ROLE EXPECTATIONS

JOB DESCRIPTIONS and role clarification are similar in that both deal with the way a person fulfills his or her ministry, and both necessitate a certain amount of negotiating with other members of the team.

Job descriptions basically list functions — who a person is involved with, to whom he reports, and his various activities. While job descriptions tend to deal in organizational and legal terms, role clarification deals more with relationships, attitudes, feelings, and expectations. While a job description will allow one to ignore tasks and people, cut around obligations, and sidestep issues, role clarification lays bare what's going on inside a person, how he feels about his ministry and the people with whom he ministers. It deals with the whole organization within which he moves. Role clarification will actually solidify a team, while a job description only suggests how a team is supposed to function.

The author prefers to work with a job description rather than without one. In numerous types of ministries over the years, I've happily worked within the framework of job descriptions. These greatly aided my effectiveness and kept the tensions at a minimum. I wish that years ago, however, I had met Myron Rush of Management Training Systems, Inc., of Colorado Springs. He introduced me to the next meaningful step beyond the job description, the concept of role clarification. I am indebted to Myron for most of the material in this chapter.

Before we take a look at how you actually go about doing a role clarification exercise, let's see the necessary prerequisites.

It's futile to go through the exercise unless your team recognizes the need and wishes to improve staff relationships. Too often staff relationships reach the breaking point before the team is willing to sit down and go through the exercise. That's human nature. Many marriage problems could be solved if a couple would take the time to go through a marital relationship enrichment clinic or retreat. A church staff that regularly goes through such an experience not only strengthens their total team output, but greatly enriches their own lives and relationships.

As a consultant to hundreds of churches during the past twenty years, there often seemed little hope of resolving the conflicts or of stopping the decline in the effectiveness of many of those ministries. If the churches had opened themselves to an evaluation on a regular basis, the decline might have been minimal.

No organization, including the church, is ever stagnant. It moves along, sometimes in an obscure way, but it moves all the same. Sometimes the church's leadership begins to lag behind the needs of its people. So a church must change the job descriptions in order to adequately serve the people's needs.

First Church in a large midwestern city had three team members. The pastor loved to counsel and was good at it. He encouraged his youth pastor to get training in the field, so that he could assist in the heavy counseling load. They hired another youth pastor to care for the youth. During that time two significant changes occurred. The college graduates no longer felt at home in the college group. And the shift of the senior and youth pastors to a heavy counseling load left a vacuum in the church administrative affairs. No one was giving oversight to the many necessary administrative tasks. This caused sufficient friction to strangle the growth of the church. This church could have saved itself a great deal of trouble by going through a role clarification exercise.

The Role Clarification Process

Set up a meeting with the team to explain the role clarifying process. Then determine if the team is ready to go through with the plans.

It is important to get away from the church facility, even out of town if possible. The participants must be free from calling the church, and especially from running back to the office to care for the ever-pressing ministry affairs. Because it takes concentration by each team member to carry through with the exercise, it is wise to make a physical break with the church and its people. Nothing but extreme emergencies should interfere.

Start during an evening hour, with supper together. Some slowing-down time could be a significant factor in preparing everyone's minds for the days and hours to follow. A short explanation of the process and its advantages, and a time for team members to express their fears are the only major business items which need to be cared for during the first session.

Some advantages of a role clarification session are:

1. Communication among the team will open up.
2. People will think about current needs and situations that may have been neglected for some time.
3. Team members will find that key areas of the ministry which have been neglected will now fit into the proper framework and be given sufficient time and energy.
4. There will be delight in reviewing progress which has occurred in recent months.
5. Information about the people, the programs, and the ministry as a whole can be communicated.
6. Touchy issues, which were untouchable in the past, will be dealt with and these pressures released.
7. The session should be a problem solver. For instance, the group may find some much needed, newly defined job descriptions coming out of the work session.

Each time the staff members go through the role clarification process, they will find it much easier. In a sense, the first session will set the pace for those which follow. The first evening, explain the whole process in capsule form. You will gather the information from the lengthy, more complete description which follows here.

Facing the Risks

When team members realize the risk involved in going through the process, they may be reluctant to follow through with the plans. Therefore, ask every team member to write down the fears he/she has about being engaged in the role clarifying exercises. Assure the group that this session is to be non-judgmental. You can expect such statements as: "I don't want to face the pain of revealing all of my insecurity in relation to my role on the team." "I have some feelings about other team members that I don't feel free to express." "I'm afraid I will not be accepted when I'm totally honest." "My job may turn out to be something I didn't want it to be." "I'm afraid some things which will be said may be detrimental to our team's future relationships." "I'm reluctant to change." "I'm uncertain how I'm going to respond to unknown pressures which may be put upon me through this exercise."

Encourage everyone to be totally honest with feelings. If the members are not, the meeting could be a waste of time. It will be a great help to everyone to get his or her fears out in the open. The moderator should review those fears and try to alleviate as many of them as possible.

After team members have discussed their fears, have each one identify what he expects to gain from this retreat. It is just as important to discuss these expectations as it is to discuss fears. If the members go into the role clarification process with false expectations, they will become frustrated.

Now it's time to discuss whether everyone wants to go through with the exercise. If you do not have one hundred percent agreement, working through the process will not be effective. Everyone must be involved and excited about the outcome. The new role expectations will be effective only if each person has had a certain input. The total new relationship is like a puzzle and everyone holds a piece. The picture won't be complete unless each piece is put in place.

It's possible that you may not get one hundred percent agreement even after you have gone this far. You may need to take a second look, and maybe even a third, before everyone is ready to enter into the process. You may need to postpone the exercise until everyone is agreed about doing so.

The Facilitator's Role

You've had a long enough glance at the process to realize how critical is the role of the moderator. Of course, if you have a trained professional, the whole process will run smoother. However, it is possible to use someone who isn't trained in the process but who is experienced in good communication and who understands group dynamics.

The moderator, first of all, must be from outside the team. He or she could be a member of the church, but that isn't recommended since a church member will have some vested interest and/or a special friendship with some member of the team. Naturally, one of the staff members cannot be the leader at this point, since his role is also up for review. No doubt a teacher, a professor, a pastor from another church who is not a close friend of one of the staff, or a business person who may have handled personnel problems at his place of employment could serve as moderator. If only male members serve on the team, it would be wise to have a male facilitator. Choose the moderator carefully because he holds the whole deck of cards in his hands. If the cards aren't dealt properly, one or more of the team may back off from being honestly involved.

The moderator should see himself as a facilitator who will not seek to identify the roles or even tell the team how the roles should be developed. He will simply get them started and make sure they don't get bogged down in the process. If the group seems to be floundering, or if the discussion becomes too intense, he may want to call for a recess, so the members have time to think for awhile about what's going on. An effective moderator should know how to keep the group moving in a happy and profitable fashion. He will guide the team's contributions to the discussion in such a way as to facilitate the process, but will never let the team members gang up on the person whose role is being examined.

Negotiating Role Expectations

The moderator will start with the senior pastor. He will remind the pastor that he is in charge of negotiating his own role, just as each other staff member will do when his turn comes. The pastor's session will be finished when he has satisfactorily clarified his own role. He will work at it until he feels comfortable enough with his role that he can work within its framework. Before that conversation is completed, everyone on the team should come to a unanimous decision about what the role of the senior pastor should be. That is going to take a great deal of honesty on the part of the whole team.

Each team member will write down what he conceives the senior pastor's role to be at this present time. This means that everyone must forget past job descriptions and roles. In light of where the church is currently, what should be the role of the pastor? The team members will look at each position as if they are forming the position in relation to the present needs and conditions of the organization. This will take a minimum of thirty minutes and could take as long as an hour.

Now the senior pastor will post his sheet and will clarify it for the rest of the team. Only after he has done this will the other team members post their sheets and clarify or interpret what they conceive his role to be.

The moderator will take notes on any disagreements. It could seem as minor as the need for the pastor to play a greater role in encouraging the Sunday school staff, or as major as the pastor leading the elder board in the development of a shepherding program or building a new sanctuary.

Now the major arbitration gets underway. When the pastor sees on the other team members' sheets what he hasn't included, he will discuss with them those differences. They will negotiate back and forth until there is either an agreement or until the idea is discarded.

The moderator may keep a low profile if the discussion is moving along smoothly and he senses that everyone is being honest and kind. He may throw a question into the discussion periodically either to clarify a point or to add another issue which isn't being considered. Like a judge on the bench in a courtroom, he can ask any person's comments to be clarified, or he can make a judgment that a certain comment is unjust or rudely spoken. If the persons involved are not clarifying the various points, the moderator will ask them to give specific illustrations of how they see their point actually being carried out. The object of the whole process is to make sure that everyone understands each point.

As the discussion moves along, a much deeper trust and appreciation should be developing on the part of each member. Fellow workers are no doubt going to learn that they were far more respected than they had thought, or they may learn to their dismay that what they thought was a successful program was just the opposite.

When the senior pastor's role is completed, each team member in turn will go through the same process. You will probably want to decide in advance in what order to work through the staff members' roles. This could be done by drawing straws, by seniority, or even by birthdates. The pecking order of the staff in certain churches may influence who's going to be considered when.

Part II: **Functioning of a Team**

8

MANAGING UPWARD

"Are you crazy? We've used my old system for years!"

8

MANAGING UPWARD

OVER THE YEARS I have found myself being a garbage can. People "dump" a lot of things on me. That often happens to a consultant, especially when he is not directly involved in their churches. People in the congregation talk to me when I'm in their homes. Most often it's about one or more of their staff members. But staff members, in various degrees of politeness also tell me about other vocational staff members on their team.

Pastors tell me how lazy their associates are, how they have no vision, or how inept their team members are. I need to listen carefully to see if this is a cover-up for their own weaknesses. Maybe the pastors are jealous because they aren't in the spotlight, or maybe they are failing and it's easier to blame the other team members than to take the blame for the failure themselves.

Without question, there is just as much complaining, or "dumping," if not more so, on the part of the other staff members about their pastor. Again, some of the complaints are well-founded, and other times they are not. The frustration level seems to be the highest here, because the staff members feel there is little they can do to solve the problems. The pastor is generally seen as the boss, and bosses are expected to evaluate, chasten, or fire, if necessary.

Whoever heard of subordinates bossing, or managing, their bosses? Take heart, there is such a thing. We call it managing upward. One of the real proofs that a team is a genuine team is that managing upward can and does take place.

Misconceptions About Managing Upward

Before managing upward is possible, team members must overcome general *misconceptions* about the idea.

1. *Subordinates don't have a right to manage upward.* That would be too risky or arrogant. It would appear to be manipulation.

   Keep in mind, however, that manipulation is doing something for your own benefit. If what you are doing is for the benefit of the church as a whole, it is motivation.
2. *It isn't the responsibility of the subordinate to manage.* The team leader has the responsibility of managing the team members.

   Actually, a genuine team allows for the give and take to flow both ways.
3. *A younger person shouldn't manage an older person.* The younger members of the team should always respect the older members for their years of experience. But sometimes practice doesn't make perfect, it merely makes one consistent. Unfortunately, it may mean years of consistently doing something wrong, or doing it poorly. Also, times change, and what worked in the past may not be working now. The young people have a great deal to teach us. Some of my greatest lessons have been learned from sensitive, wise, and loving, but much younger, members of the body of Christ.
4. *Stern, authoritative leaders are unwilling to take suggestions from others.* They are the "Indian chiefs," and even their wives or board members can't seem to move them.

   Team members probably haven't seen an occasion where managing upward has overcome such a situation, so they don't know how to go about it. But even this type of leader will often respond if approached properly.

   If a leader proves impossible to change, the staff person may need to live with the conflict, or seek another position. Before accepting this ultimatum, be sure you have first tried carefully all of the options suggested in the last half of this chapter.

Need for Managing Upward

1. *The team needs regular staff meetings.* A staff can't be a team without a staff meeting any more than a football team can play a game without a huddle. A busy pastor either can't see the need, or can't find the time in his demanding schedule, to call those weekly staff meetings. His associate feels alone and out of the flow of the church's

ministry, because there is no set time for communication and for the blending of their lives together for a team ministry. Years of listening and observing tells me that this is probably the number one need for managing upward.

2. *The team needs checkpoints.* We don't like to admit it, but we all have our blind spots. Often they cost us far more in our effectiveness than we would really like to know. One of the greatest benefits of a team is that we have a checkpoint in our system. A man who tells me that he takes his orders only from the Lord is really admitting that he can't stand to be evaluated. Evaluation needs to flow both up and down. It's best when the senior pastor initiates the process, but more often than not the associate sees and feels the need and probably should manage that upward also. This problem will surface when the pastor has his first associate, or when there is an age gap between the two.
3. *The team needs a leader.* Leadership skills are required for such projects as planning the year's calendar, time and people management, setting goals for the church, and determining each team member's ministry. Team members desire a voice in the decision-making process. The associate feels this need the most, because he is evaluated by the congregation more than is the pastor. The associate's hands are tied unless the pastor takes the lead, or at least gives his support to new visions, goals, or strategies. So the associate strongly feels the need to manage upward.
4. *The team needs to share.* This is perhaps the most sensitive, and thus the most difficult to pull off. I call it life sharing. If the senior pastor is fifty or older, he is not likely to be open to sharing his inner struggles and emotions. That seems to be a more recent phenomenon. Yet to develop a sense of intimacy, a sense of oneness, which is essential to team ministry, sharing must take place. The true blending of hearts and minds together in sharing and prayer may often need to be initiated by the associate.
5. *The team needs to disciple the congregation.* Each member must aid the pastor in his people ministry. This may be called discipling people or shepherding the flock. The pastor may be a strong operational manager and/or preacher and may not feel comfortable or capable with his relational skills. Yet the associate hears from the congregation that the members would like to have the

pastor disciple them. The associate hears the need, sees it himself, and may have the ability to do so. But he doesn't know how to get the pastor moving in that direction. That calls for managing upward.

Procedure for Managing Upward

If you are the senior pastor in your church and are reading this book, you are by this time already practicing some of the procedures for managing upward. As the leader, you will give each member of your team opportunity to evaluate both new and existing programs. Concentrate on evaluating one project at a time.

Begin with positive comments, pointing out what went well. Be lavish with compliments. Approach problems with the idea of how similar situations can be handled in the future. Be sure to keep negative comments constructive and relevant to the program itself. Remember that you are evaluating the program, not the person or his total ministry.

The rest of this chapter is written from the viewpoint of the associate minister. If you are the senior pastor and have difficulty promoting changes with members of your team, with your church boards, or with leaders in your congregation, adapt these suggestions accordingly.

If you are an associate working with an unresponsive pastor, the next few pages are for you.

So you are going to be courageous and seek to manage upward. It may come easily, but more likely you will need to be consistent, tenacious, and gentle. A wise husband or wife knows that there are certain times when it is appropriate, and other times when it is not appropriate, to approach certain subjects. A wise change agent, or upward manager, has that sense of timing. When things are generally going right, there is less pressure than normal and plenty of time to discuss all the issues at hand. You have carefully thought through all the issues and your approach is well designed. Now you are ready to choose one of the following four approaches to managing upward, as suggested by James Stoner of Fordham University. I will use a case study with each one of the methods to show how this particular method might work.

A. Direct Problem Solving

1. Assess yourself and your needs.
    a. Consider your own personal strengths and weaknesses in regards to this area of needed change.

   b. Evaluate your own attitude toward authoritative figures.
   c. Evaluate your own style of leadership. Is it significantly different from your pastor's style? Can you allow him to operate with his style? Is the long range objective the real issue, or is the real issue the way the team tries to get the mission done?
2. Seek to understand your pastor and his context.
   a. Do you know what his goals and expectations are?
   b. What are his weaknesses, blind spots, and strengths as they relate to the issue at hand?
   c. Evaluate the workstyle of team members. How can the problem at hand be worked out within that style?
3. Shop for the best plan to implement the required change.
   a. Research the various ways that reliable organizations and churches go about dealing with this need.
   b. Use your best problem solving skills to improve the relationships involved.
4. Lay out clearly the problem-solving steps for the pastor.
   a. Be flexible and open to any changes in the plan that he would like to add.
   b. Design the steps that each will take to see the plan implemented.
   c. Set the next time when you will evaluate the progress together.

John is the pastor of a growing church in a western college town. He is an effective forty-two-year-old preacher. He likes to spend time with the collegians and has led many of them to a saving knowledge of Christ. His sessions with the church board are given to dealing with church problems and program plans. When Steve came as the Christian Education Director, he became effective in discipling some of the church's educational leaders. Numerous elders asked that he do the same with them. Why hadn't the pastor discipled the leaders before? Steve's task was to help the pastor undertake that needed ministry. How could he manage that part of the pastor's life and ministry?

After many weeks of contemplation and prayer, Steve decided to talk to John about an idea for helping the new college converts grow in Christ, and, at the same time, develop spiritual maturity in the elders. He knew John deeply wanted both of these. If the elders were discipled, they in turn could disciple the new college converts. Since Steve knew the elders respected John so much, he knew they would love to see him involved in their lives. He stressed these facts in his approach. Steve asked John for help in the skills needed to implement a discipleship program, since he had never been discipled himself. They worked on the approach John would use when they met for their weekly staff sessions. In a year's time the focus of the monthly board meetings had shifted to discipleship.

B. Shaping Behavior

1. Clarify exactly what behavior you would like to see changed. Make sure that the motivation for the change is for his and the church's good, and not for your own convenience.
2. Respond on a repeated basis positively to any signs of appropriate action by your pastor. Basically you will be practicing positive reinforcement.
3. Positive reinforcement on your part keeps you from responding negatively to the opposite behavior. At the same time you will work hard not to respond negatively to the desired action.

Pastor Peters is a most gregarious, relational-style manager. He is always available to the congregation whenever the members drop by. Because he is so busy with the flock, he has difficulty finding the needed time to study, and consequently little if any time for planning. Many things are done poorly, and many things are left totally undone. Many of the church officers in the congregation are looking to him for leadership. But even more so is the new Christian Education Director, Delbert Meeker. Much of his success is dependent on the leadership of the pastor. Because Delbert is a strong operational manager, he is quick to see the failure of Pastor Peters' lack of goal setting and planning. He sees that the people run the pastor's life and ministry and he has little time to run the church.

Delbert's effort to manage upward showed itself in the compliments he gave the pastor for the small efforts he made in planning a series of sermons during the Christmas season, and for a new effort to bring variety to the worship service. Delbert was quick to point out the benefits that occurred from such planning. Although the new year came and went without any plans for outreach and new programming, Delbert held his tongue. He simply went about setting as many plans as he could for his part of the program and, without too much fanfare, let Mr. Peters see the benefits of his own planning. In time Mr. Peters slowly started to implement plans for other parts of the church's mission.

C. Setting an Example

1. Choose an activity in which you want your pastor to initiate or improve, and where you can provide a good model.
2. Plan thoroughly and execute well so that the pastor can see how it should be completed. Be cautious so that you do not execute it in such a fashion as to show up the pastor.
3. When you have finished, ask the pastor to make comments on the model. Again, be careful not to say, "Well, look what I've done, now tell me how good it was." Your attitude should be, "Was this said or done in such a way that it was effective, or was it ineffective?" You may even go so far as to ask if he would feel comfortable in doing the same.

This approach might help your pastor become more open with his attitudes and feelings. It might also encourage him to suggest an evaluation of some of his programs.

Elmer had been at Elmgrove Church for only a year, but he was well aware that the senior minister was not open to evaluation on any of his sermons or various ministries. Elmer knew that he himself was young and inexperienced, but others in the congregation had similar feelings about the pastor's task. Elmer was asked to be in charge of the evening church service on the fourth Sunday of September. He decided this would be a great time to launch the fall youth program. He would make it a youth night.

Elmer planned thoroughly with all his team, but at the same time he was laying plans to ask the pastor for a thorough evaluation at the following staff meeting. He made sure there was time on the agenda for the evaluation. He started the evaluation by talking about how much he appreciated the team's work, and stated what his objectives were in presenting the program. He asked the senior pastor to give him an honest critique about how effective those goals had been. He was careful not to be defensive about any corrective comments. He thanked the pastor for the insights and expressed gratitude that he could learn to be more effective on another occasion because of these insights.

After following the same procedure with numerous events, the pastor asked Elmer for his evaluation on his last series of sermons. You may need to risk asking for the honor of evaluating the pastor's ministry after a period of time, if he does not follow your lead.

D. Moving Toward Negotiating Change

1. Select something you are convinced needs a change and which you are willing to seek to change.
2. Plan carefully the strategy necessary to bring about the change.
3. Inform the pastor of your desire to make the change, and all the logical and spiritual reasons why the change ought to be made.
4. Request feedback from the pastor and be ready to negotiate any alterations in that plan.
   a) Your willingness to adapt should make him agreeable to implementing these changes.
   b) You need to be ready to compromise any segment of your original strategy so that the final plan will be mutually agreeable.
   c) Make sure he agrees that the planned change is mutually beneficial to all parties concerned, and that it is honestly beneficial to the edification of the body of Christ.
5. Set the exact date and strategy for implementing the plan. Set a termination date for its completion and make sure that each step of the plan is specifically assigned to each person.

This approach to managing upward is especially useful in establishing new programs, changing approaches to ministry, and developing a regular structured staff meeting.

Pastor Don Drielling started Jewell Avenue Reformed Church, and after ten years it had grown to a regular attendance of 600, with three staff members. When Jim, the third staff member, joined the team, Don felt there was a need to hold weekly staff meetings. Everything went fine the first three months. However, the constant demands of a growing congregation continued to crowd in on the busy schedule, and the first thing to go was the staff meeting. Somehow they could get along without that time for communion and communication. Tensions began to build and details dropped between the cracks. When Jim saw what was happening, he decided it was time for upward management.

Jim asked for a meeting with Pastor Don to explain how important it was for the staff to be together weekly. They discussed how it would ultimately help to strengthen their team work and thus make their ministry more effective. They laid out a plan that would keep other events from robbing them of that hallowed session. It would be placed on the weekly calendar and the secretary would not allow other things to be scheduled at the same time. Jim wanted more time for each session, but he was willing to meet for a shorter period of time. The schedule necessitated him giving up another special weekly event which he deemed less important. They agreed that Jim would be given the opportunity to call the meeting if Pastor Don failed to do so. Now he, too, became successful at managing upward.

Managing upward is a lot like disciplining your children. The same method of discipline doesn't work with each one of your children and doesn't always work each time you try it. Good team members are like good parents. They don't give up easily, because they see how critical it is to obtain their objective. Keep trying different approaches until you find the one that works. If you are committed to a team ministry, you are committed to either the receiving or the giving side of managing upward.

Part III: **Maintaining the Team**

9

THE STAFF MEETING

"I've made up my mind, would you still like to discuss this issue?"

9

THE STAFF MEETING

WHEN A FOOTBALL team runs onto the field, the players have a game plan clearly in mind. The game plan is built on certain suppositions about their team skills, how they best function together. The players have a fairly clear picture of their opponent — what the team members' strengths and weaknesses are, and what chance they have of defeating them. Out of those suppositions come their goals for that game. They anticipate that they will win by scoring so many points. In light of all that, they design their game plan, or strategy.

During the first half of the game, all of those principles have been challenged. "Well, what are your plans in the second half, Coach? Are you going to stick to the game plan?" The interviewer is basically asking the coach where he was off in his suppositions, goals, or strategies in the first half. A coach becomes a great coach because at the halftime he knows how to make shifts necessary in the game plan in order to reach their goal of winning.

In many ways a staff meeting is like the half-time locker room meeting of a team. No sensible coach would sell his rights to the team meeting. It may make all the difference in the outcome of his efforts. Yet, how tragic to see some lead pastors not even bothering to take advantage of their staff meetings where in essence the same purposes are to be accomplished.

The church coach may once in awhile come up with the same comment a coach does. "Well, we'll just stay with the same game plan, but here is how we are going to do it next week." All the same emotions may be felt in a locker room as in a board meeting, where the staff huddles each week. It's a place to laugh, cry, and work through depression or disappointment. It is a time to deal with your bad feelings toward those who let you down, or to stroke the players who made outstanding plays. How can a team be a team without those critical huddles?

Having been a member of seven different teams, including church staff teams, state and national denominational teams, and the team of a seminary, I have observed and worked with hundreds of others.This convinced me that if Satan wants to destroy the work of Christ's body, he will first attack the staff, because that is the root of its strength. It's like cutting out the root of a tree and expecting it to live. The best place to preserve the unity and destroy the enemy is in the staff meeting. Without a regular team meeting, you are opening up yourself to our enemy's first line of attack.

In recent years, I have watched and studied a model staff in Denver. The South Evangelical Presbyterian Fellowship, although not large, is known for the dynamic spiritual growth of its congregation. The staff practices the microcosm concept better than any other I've observed. All the good things I have practiced on a team, or at times wished could have happened on a team are practiced on this team. The staff is not perfect, nor will it always be as strong as it currently is. But it will be a model for developing your team.

I am grateful to them for letting me observe, study, and question their practices so we can all benefit. I will use their philosophy and agenda as a guide for the rest of the chapter, but I will sprinkle throughout illustrations from other churches and experiences. Their philosophy is constantly being updated and revised.

South Evangelical Presbyterian Fellowship's church philosophy statement, included in the Appendix of this book, has served as a springboard for its staff philosophy. You will see the similarities. You will also note that the staff's agenda flows out of its philosophy and is a means to its accomplishment.

Staff Philosophy

1. We are the people of God before we are the servants of God.

If you try to run a church like a business, you overlook the fact that a church is primarily an organism and not an organization. Since the staff is a reflection of the body, then the organism's concept should be foundational to its operation.

A staff must come to the place where the members first and always look upon each other as spiritual beings who maintain an ongoing relationship with each other as unified members of the body of Christ. That thought will greatly alter the working relationship of the team members toward each other. South Evangelical Fellowship's staff believes this so deeply that their first agenda item each week is an hour together in the intimate body-life experience of sharing and worship. The staff is divided into small groups which periodically reorganize. The members share their personal concerns, encourage one another, discuss steps of spiritual growth, and pray for each other. This paves the way for a smooth and harmonious business session which follows. This is also a good model for the church board. Seeing each other first as God's people will then affect the way we perceive each team member as he fulfills his role.

2. We share our personal lives together.

Genuine *koinonia* is the basic root that ties the body together. We will have a hard time fulfilling God's designed oneness for us without sharing our whole lives with each other, both the spiritual and social parts of our personhood.

Many team members find it essential to participate with their fellow team members in extra-curricular activities, so they will get to know each other as whole people, not just impersonal workers on an assembly line. Some find this fulfillment in casual luncheons, attending entertaining programs together, or competing in athletic events.

The whole South Evangelical Fellowship staff enjoys a family potluck on a rotating basis in various members' homes so that the staff members can get to know each other and their families. This helps them understand each other better. Beware of one pitfall, however. I've noticed that when two members build a coalition together to the exclusion of other team members, it's most often done by building a friendship in an extra-curricular activity. To avoid this problem, plan get-togethers with various members of the team.

3. We are committed to the whole church's ministry, rather than to our individual ministry. We see everyone and every part as equally important.

South Evangelical Fellowship's career minister testified to the fact that each success or failure was not individualized, but was considered the success or failure of the whole team. It is obvious in their planning and evaluations that they are totally committed to each other's success.

To realize this total commitment, plan time to listen to each other's dreams and goals. Participate in their planning. When this happens, you multiply the total effectiveness of the team's ministry, resulting in geometric success.

4. We concentrate on a common philosophy of ministry. A friend at the Institute of Church Imperatives in Modesto, California, asked staff members in different departments about their philosophy. He was amazed to get the same answers from all of them. No decision is made without honestly asking whether that particular decision is a reflection of their priorities and philosophy statement. They have made strong commitments to that philosophy and this keeps them from wasting energy. They are all going in the same direction. This is especially important because a church can't do everything, even if it has many staff members. The philosophy guards the priorities. So, if your church is committed to a ministry to families, that means that your youth minister, as well as your family relations minister, keeps that in focus.

5. We work on a consensus rather than on a majority. To a highly structured person, consensus is a sloppy and ineffective way of doing things. If your team is comprised of twenty or more, you may need to vote periodically. But consensus has great things going for it which should be considered.

First, it greatly affects the atmosphere of the meeting. Formality will often keep people from speaking their deep feelings and convictions, which in turn can destroy your sense of oneness. Open attitudes are encouraged when you operate by consensus.

Second, consensus results in accepting and still loving those who hold out against the majority. You will respect this procedure more when you live with it a while. Often the one or two who hold out against the others had more insight and may save you from a tremendous mistake. Even though you are operating in a freer style, you should continue to record your decisions in a formal manner.

Third, stronger rationale for consensus voting is that it places more responsibility upon each member for each decision which is made.

For example, your staff may be wrestling with the idea of changing the time for your evening service. If Jonathan is the only one holding out for not changing the time, he must think more seriously about his decision. The weight of that decision rests upon his shoulders. Is he truly objective about the decision he is making for the whole team? Does he have any hidden agendas which he isn't free to share? Although there is no guarantee, a defensive, negative person's attitude is altered when he realizes that his decision is respected by the others. Note this idea from Lester DeKoster.

> "The Quakers have an interesting way of arriving at corporate decisions. As a visiting teacher, I sat through some discussions in a Quaker college faculty. At the point where a chairman would normally declare the discussion ended and call for the vote, the Quakers often lay a matter on the table. 'We are not ready,' they say, 'to make a decision. The Spirit needs more time to work. Better left open than ill-decided.'
>
> What the Quakers seek is consensus; if not unanimity, then as close to it as possible. They know, of course, that matters cannot hang fire indefinitely, and Quaker success in business enterprise suggests that at least some of their people know how to seize a conclusion and run with it. But for a visitor, the process is endlessly fascinating. Every facet gets discussed, and sometimes one can almost feel the forming of a common mind, the shift in sentiment, the opening of new perspective. If democracy is long in making up its mind, then Quaker democracy is often tortoise slow. Small matter, they will say, if the truth is found at last.
>
> The significance of this Quaker experience is the light it sheds on a little game that is played in some non-Quaker churches. I am thinking of the growing practice of electing women as 'adjunct' deacons or elders, and including these as members in council meetings.
>
> I call it a game, because the pretense is that the 'adjunct' does not vote, and therefore does not really exercise authority in the congregation. I have long supposed that those who argue this way cannot be really serious, but new examples of the argument crop up just the same.
>
> This argument assumes precisely what the Quaker knows to be false, namely the assumption that influence comes to expression only in the final vote. Not at all. The whole Quaker process illumines exactly the opposite, and in this is undoubtedly correct. What a vote does is simply summarize where the group has come through the discussion that preceded the balloting. What matters is that discussion. And whoever is entitled to participate in that discussion does exert an influence upon the outcome. This is no doubt why church council meetings are not free-for-alls with anyone who drops by taking part.
>
> Were this not so, then all that is said about the virtues of democracy (and there are many) would rest upon a misconception. Then delegates to a national convention might as well stay at home and mail in their votes. Then election campaigns are not only tedious, but in fact are totally unnecessary. Let each voter go cold and uninformed to the polling booth and vote his view of the moment.

The fact is that participation in discussion leading to decision is the way to democracy's superiority over totalitarianism. This is the ground for a free press and politically uncontrolled news media.

And, accordingly, participation in council or consistory discussions is involvement in church administration. Of course!

It is hard to believe that advocates of 'adjunct' office bearers can themselves take seriously the argument that abstention from voting at the end of a discussion process exempts anyone from influence upon the process, and upon that final vote.

When the worldly play games, they are, after all, true to character. When the churchly do the same, what is to be said of them?" — Lester DeKoster, *Playing Games with Decision Making.*

6. We see differences as strengths in personalities.

The larger the staff becomes, obviously the greater the diversity in personalities. Consequently, the greater the potential for misunderstanding and conflict. As you saw in Part II, a strong staff will actually seek diversity because it brings a much broader perspective on any one issue. In order for a staff to benefit from diversity, the members remind themselves of the benefit in diversity, because often it will seem like a negative factor.

Don't allow those differences to cause a sense of distrust to develop among the staff. Because another person sees an issue through the unique grid of his personality, it will be easy to distrust the other person's observations and recommendations. Remember that perfect love, which ought to be a guide for the operation of the team, "does not seek its own, bears all things, believes all things and endures all things".

The South Evangelical Fellowship's staff has a Director of Women's Ministries. A member of the team commented on the advantage of a woman's perspective on various issues. Women tend to be more subjective, while men tend to be more objective on most issues. Fortunately, certain men's personalities move toward a subjective temperament as well. When you have a whole team of objective people making decisions that will affect a mixed congregation, it's important to have both extremes represented.

First Peter 3:7 suggests that husbands are to live with their wives in an understanding way, lest the answer to their prayers be hindered. If husbands don't take into consideration the uniqueness of women's ways, or thought processes, that can be an actual factor in hindering their prayers. Although the passage doesn't refer to a church staff, the same principle is true. Seek to be patient, understanding, and respectful for the uniqueness of the other team members, so the power of prayer will not be withdrawn from the staff.

7. We believe that it can't happen through us until it happens to us.

Only this point and the first one are in chronological order. The other points make it possible for this point to be effective. Each staff member should play a key role in the other person's spiritual development and in his or her ministry's effectiveness. The members will be "provoking" or "stimulating one another into love and good works" (Heb. 10:24). Each should draw out the others productivity. When the team's lives are interacting with one another in the body, they have the potential for developing excellence in spiritual ministry.

One of a staff member's greatest dangers is that he will lead a segment of the congregation in a spiritual exercise because it is expected of him, even though he has not experienced the same reality himself. The pastor cannot lead his congregation through his preaching to a spiritual level which he has not experienced. The same is true for each team member, as he or she seeks to guide portions of the congregation in various spiritual exercises.

Staff Meeting Agenda

South Evangelical Fellowship's agenda serves as a model for us to study. Comments and illustrations will be added from other churches.

1. 8:00-9:00 A.M. — *Groups of sharing, study, and prayer.* This time is very personal and is a group worship experience. The small groups change personnel from time to time to allow for total group interaction. Of course, a smaller staff would always meet together. This could be a time to share experiences each staff member is having in his or her personal walk with the Lord.
2. 9:00-10:00 A.M. — *Staff relations.* In this time slot, the whole staff studies together. I agree with Fred Smith of Dallas that people who aren't interested in studying and interacting with new thoughts won't be making dynamic creative contributions to the team effort. The following studies will help cement the hearts and minds of the staff together.

   a) A study of the "one another passages." Ask each member to choose the "one anothers" of his own interest, ones he can see himself practicing. Take as many weeks as necessary, building a practical profile of the ways staff members see these being lived out in their team.

The One Anothers	*Passage*	*What Does It Mean?*
1. Members of One Another	Romans 12:5	
2. Devoted to One Another	Romans 12:10	
3. Honor One Another	Romans 12:10	
4. Be of the Same Mind With One Another	Romans 15:5; 12:16	
5. Accept One Another	Romans 15:7	
6. Admonish One Another	Romans 15:14	
7. Greet One Another	Romans 16:3-6, 16	
8. Serve One Another	Galatians 5:13	
9. Bear One Another's Burdens	Galatians 6:2	
10. Bearing With One Another	Ephesians 4:2	
11. Submit to One Another	Ephesians 5:21	
12. Encourage One Another	1 Thessalonians 5:11	

b) Do a study of spiritual gifts to help the members on the team determine which ones they possess. You may choose to use a text to aid you in this study, such as:
Spiritual Gifts and Church Growth Modified Questionaire — Charles E. Fuller Institute of Evangelism and Church Growth
Trenton Spiritual Gifts Analysis — Fuller Institute of Pasadena
A Practical Guide to Finding Your Spiritual Gifts
Tim Blanchard — Tyndale House Publishers
Spiritual Gifts

Bobby Clinton — World Team Missions
Gifts of the Spirit
Ronald E. Baxter — Kregel Publications

c) Do a study of the qualifications of a leader as seen in Titus, and 1 Peter and 1 Timothy. Examine each other in light of these lists.

Passage	*Characteristic*	*What Does It Mean?*
1 Timothy 3:2-7	Above reproach	
	Husband of one wife	
	Temperate	
	Prudent	
	Respectable	
	Hospitable	
	Able to teach	
	Not addicted to wine	
	Not pugnacious	
	Gentle	
	Uncontentious	
	Free from the love of money	
	Manages his own household well	
	Keeps children under control with dignity	
	Not a new convert	
	Good reputation with non-believers	
Titus 1:6-9	Having children who believe	
	Not self-willed	
	Not quick-tempered	
	Not fond of sordid gain	
	Loving what is good	
	Sensible	
	Just	
	Devout	

Passage	*Characteristic*	*What Does It Mean?*
Titus 1:6-9, cont.	Self-controlled	
	Holds fast the Word	
	Exhorts in sound doctrine	
	Refutes those who contradict	
1 Peter 5:2-3	Ability to shepherd	
	Shepherding voluntarily	
	Eagerness in ministry	
	Not lording over others	
	Example to the flock	

d) The South Evangelical Fellowship staff members each read and then interacted with the helpful workbook, *The Truth About You,* by Mattson and Revell. This is a useful guide to opening greater potential for each person's gifts and abilities, which in turn builds the team.

e) Another helpful study would be the use of the Management Training Systems Temperament Analysis Test. After each person has taken the test, have a discussion on how the team best can utilize the members management skills in building the body of Christ. Don't forget that Christ has given to the church gifted men and women to direct or manage the spiritual exercise of the saints (Eph. 4:10-12).

f) This would be a great time to study theological issues which require interpretation based on Scripture. These could include current issues of concern to church life and thought, such as our stand on divorce and remarriage, the use of alcoholic beverages, baptism without church membership, decision making and the will of God, what we as a church can and should do about social concerns, how to enrich the ministry of evangelism and discipleship, and what we regard to be the signs of spiritual growth.

g) What about a study on the fruits of the spirit? I agree with Joe Bayley when he says that "we should be studying the fruit of the Spirit more than the gifts of the Spirit." It seems as if the church suffers more from the lack of fruit, than from failure to use the gifts.

3. 10:00-11:00 A.M. — *Business.* Here is another occasion to express the unity and operation of the team. Report what is going on in each ministry. Since each person has played a role in the decision-making process, he will certainly want to know what has happened in the various areas the past week.

Include discussion of the public worship services. It is our recommendation that the whole staff reflect not only on the meaningfulness of each part of the worship service, but also on the preaching. Since the pastor confirms and corrects the other team members' contributions to the corporate work of the staff, he should encourage recommendations concerning his sermons. If he wants only affirmations of his preaching, he can kill the team spirit. Some pastors haven't been critiqued since seminary, and since then haven't corrected their bad preaching manners, or have developed other bad habits. Nothing will open others to correction quicker than being open yourself. In all cases keep criticism constructive and in line with the personality of the individual.

Fred Smith in the Fall, 1982 issue of *Leadership Journal* makes an interesting comment about people he'd like on his team. "I want a person who is comfortable being reviewed regularly . . . In a Christian setting, many staff members resist review. They feel they have been called of God, and therefore the pastor or the department head is not really their supervisor—God is. If their concept of what God wants them to do (which is usually what they happen to enjoy doing) conflicts with what the organization expects of them, it is too bad for the organization. Such an attitude brings havoc into the work force of the kingdom. I want people in my organization who are subject to review, who receive it willingly, and who profit from it."

Before a staff member presents a proposal to the team for consideration, he should think through all the reasons why his idea should be accepted. What objections will other team members make? If he hasn't thought through this in advance, his proposal will likely be defeated. What are the various stages needed to carry out this project? He should take into consideration all the angles as he puts his final proposal into writing. The staff will need concrete facts to deal with. It will save hours of time if advanced thinking has gone into the project.

Other business matters should include the coordination of the church calendar and the discussion of any new procedures that need to be organized. Budgetary items should be on the agenda as well.

A highlight of the discussion will revolve around assignments and progress reports on ministry to members of the congregation. This will include hospital calls (who is making them), what spiritual progress is occurring in lives of individuals, what spiritual discussions are being held by people in the various discipleship programs, how leaders are functioning, who made visits last week with various prospects and members. All of these items about people are critical, since numerous staff people will interact with the same members of the congregation at different times. Pastor Jim may have discovered that the Samuelsons are currently having marital problems. The family minister was just about to ask them to take a leadership role. It was good they discussed this issue.

The agenda should be prepared in advance and it should be a reflection of the items coming up in the next weeks and months. At the bottom of each week's minutes should be a list of the assignments given to each staff member. The following week members should report on how many of those assignments were carried out.

Included here is a sample planning sheet that First Baptist Church in Modesto uses regularly to make sure all the assignments are covered. This detailed planning results in a well-run service.

Sunday Staff Assignments

9:30 A.M.	11:00 A.M.	6:30 A.M.
WORKING THE PLATFORM		
Pastor Blanc	Pastor Blanc	Pastor Blanc
Bud LaCore	Bud LaCore	Bud LaCore
John Gustafson	John Gustafson	John Gustafson
Baptism-Jon Venema	Baptism-Loyal Friesen	Baptism-Cliff
assist-Rick/Phil	assist-Cliff/Ian	assist-Henri/Manny
PHONE LINE - Back of Sanctuary - Phone 1		
Dave Langley	Cliff Sexton	Dwight Smith
INVITATION - Front of Sanctuary - Station 1		
Dave Langley	Cliff Sexton	Dwight Smith
INVITATION - Front of Sanctuary - Station 2		
Scott Ellis	Jerry Costley	Jerry Costley
INVITATION - Front of Sanctuary - Station 3		
Gary Gervase	Henri Valette	Don Wilson
INVITATION - Front of Sanctuary - Station 4		
Jim Talley	Rick Thompson	Jim Talley
SCHEDULE STAFF APPOINTMENTS		
Jerry Collins	Louis Witt	Jim Talley
USHERS, NARTHEX, BUILDINGS, AND GROUND		
Manny Mello	Dennis Chase	Rick Thompson
CUSTODIAL STAFF AUDITORIUM SIDE		
Doug Mennen	Doug Mennen	Pete Carlson
CUSTODIAL STAFF CHRISTIAN ED SIDE		
Pete Salas	Pete Salas	Melvin Berry
LIGHTING/P.A.		
Parker/Sizemore	Parker/Sizemore	Parker/Sizemore
INVITATION - All Adult Ministries staff and personnel report to back		
Wade Estes	Wade Estes	Wade Estes
Jerry Collins	Jerry Collins	Jerry Collins
Louis Witt	Louis Witt	Louis Witt
Ian Robertson	Ian Robertson	Ian Robertson
Phil Arendt		Phil Arendt
Don Ford	Don Ford	Don Ford
Chuck Smalley		Chuck Smalley
Dwight Smith	Dwight Smith	

4. 11:00—12:00 noon—*Enrichment section*. The South Evangelical Fellowship team uses this time in numerous ways, and for some teams this may seem needless. It could be used periodically rather than on a regular basis. Often a guest is brought in to teach a subject that will enrich their ministries. This may include professors from schools in the area talking about issues and trends, or it may be other church representatives who are invited to share the strengths of their church's ministry. It could be a time to view an educational video or movie, with a discussion following. It would be either theological or practical in nature.
5. 12:00—1:00 P.M.—*Lunch together*. It's possible here to further discuss the various business affairs and theological issues, or simply share casual conversations about mutual interests. This time could be used for departmental meetings.

I questioned the South Evangelical Fellowship staff about the large block of time given to the weekly staff meeting. What did their congregation feel about its length? The team members believe it takes that much time and effort to build a strong cohesive team which will become a true microcosm of the body of Christ. Even if you don't spend that much time on each section of the agenda, all the items are of equal importance. In essence that is what should happen in the body as a whole. How can they model all that the body should be if they don't give time and effort to that agenda? Some members of the congregation complained at first, until they saw the long-range effect it had on the lives of the team, and thus ultimately on the life of the church.

Settings for the staff meetings can be as critical as the agenda itself. Sociological studies indicate that our seating arrangements in a business meeting can greatly affect the way we respond. The pastor's office may not be the best setting. If his office is used he should not sit behind his desk. This would tend to give him an inordinate amount of authority. The fact that he is the chief of staff already stacks the deck in his favor, without also putting him behind the desk of authority. Even though he is not placed in an authoritative position, he should still moderate the meeting, and guide the conversation to keep it on course.

Recent studies indicate that the more authority a person

feels, the more he will interrupt others who are talking. One member of the South Evangelical Fellowship staff wanted assurance that he would be fully heard in the meetings. The moderator will aid the process, but this takes everyone's undivided attention on the person speaking. Communication is a major item in building a genuine team spirit. For example, the minister of music may have an urge to yawn when the next agenda item calls for a discussion about the youth retreat, but he should show equal interest in that as well as his Sunday evening musical. If we are yoke-fellows in the ministry, we can never consider menial any assignment in Christian service. We can project a negative attitude just by our listening stance.

When a pastor puts a low priority on the staff meeting, it can readily be set aside for another day or week which may never come. If the staff does not meet weekly, it can get out of the habit. It should be understood by everyone that the staff meeting time each week is to be guarded against instrusions. The smaller the staff, the easier it is to let interruptions destroy that sacred session. It may seem less important to a small team, because only two or three are getting together. That mind set will eat like a cancer into the team spirit, and they will soon be married singles again. Without a regular staff meeting, you will be like a group of individual soloists who belong to an orchestra, but who never have a rehearsal. They end up without harmony and no beautiful heart-lifting concert.

Numerous attitudes are held and practices are followed concerning who should attend the staff meeting. What about the secretary, the janitor, a part-time family counselor, a paid organist, or a student who serves as a part-time youth coordinator? Each chief of staff will need to decide, but these questions may need to be answered before coming to a conclusion.

A) What role do the secretaries play in the development of the team? Are they executive secretaries or simply people who type letters and answer the phone?
B) Is it possible to have various workers attend only part of the session, such as the worship time?
C) Are certain part-time staff people a major part of the planning team, or are they responsible to other middle management people on the staff?

D) Who will cover the phone while the staff is in session?
E) Will part-time team members be in the church for only a short time, and consequently not contribute to the long-range efforts and planning of the staff?

Keep in mind that each additional person who joins the sessions completely changes the group dynamics, and so you will want to think carefully who is a regular part of the staff meeting.

Your staff philosophy and agenda will be different from this model as it will reflect your uniqueness. If you wish to be a strong growing team, you will include a majority of the items which have just been discussed.

Project for Chapter 9

Staff Meeting Exercises

1. A) Have the staff compile a list of all the ingredients which comprise a healthy growing church. B) Next have the members analyze their fellowship and practice to determine what areas can be improved. C) Have the members decide how they will implement certain items which are on their master list, but which are not being practiced by their team.
2. Study Peter Wagner's and Richard Gorsuch's list of the characteristics of a quality church to be found in the *Leadership Journal*, 1983 Vol. IV, No. 1., p. 28. Check your church and staff against those lists. How do you rate? Do you agree that their list is complete? Where do you need to improve? How can your staff model a quality church where you currently are not doing so?
3. Ask for permission for one or more of your staff to visit another staff in a church in your area. Ask key questions of them which will aid you in enriching your own team meeting.

Part III: **Maintaining the Team**

10

THE STAFF RETREAT

"They're 'casting lots' to see who goes with the junior high kids to camp."

10

THE STAFF RETREAT

"A STAFF RETREAT is like refurbishing a carousel; the horses are given a coat of paint, new bulbs are screwed into banks of flashing lights, the calliope pipes are re-tuned, and the ticket-takers are given a quick course in how to run a merry-go-round. This is all done in anticipation of larger crowds who want a smooth ride and would appreciate getting off about where they got on."[1]

Maybe that doesn't sound like the retreat Jesus had with His disciples after they returned from their witnessing venture, but the effect could be somewhat the same. Jesus rehearsed with His disciples all that they had done. You can almost hear the discussion now. "I saw men smash their idols after their decision to follow Christ," Peter shouted over all the voices which seemed to be talking at once. But Thomas, with his sauntering and sullen speech, related how he was thrown out of three houses in one day in his door-to-door campaign.

Jesus saw that review and get-away time was critical to a strong life-building ministry. My observation and experience has taught me the same. In our pressurized society where there is little time to reflect on life, ministry, and our relationships, a retreat becomes almost essential to a fresh and successful service.

Remember returning from a vacation how you felt refreshed and ready to tackle the ministry with a full head of steam? After only a few days into the work, all the problems and raspy relationships were still plaguing you, just as they had before. Vacations are like retreats only in that they refresh one with new physical, emotional, and sometimes spiritual vigor to face the task. But often they don't solve problems and rebuild fractured relationships. They only shove them under the rug for awhile. Retreats with the staff, on the other hand, can build the team into that genuine microcosm, clarify goals, blend hearts, and set a new course, in addition to all the things a vacation can accomplish.

The staff of the Grove Street Church struggled all year with the decision to start a day school. Many questions needed to be answered, funds had to be raised, and additional staff had to be hired. Of course, in all that extra activity, a lot of tension built up among the staff. The problem was that only a couple of the team realized what great damage this had done to their relationships. It wasn't until they all got away together into their mountain retreat and started to evaluate the year, that they realized the existence of tattered emotions and feelings. Had they not spent those three days away, who knows how long before the cork could have blown! Going to a retreat can be like replacing the air filter in your furnace. Much hidden resistance to the flow isn't noticed until it's been cleaned or replaced.

Mark was the Music and Christian Education Director at a western suburban church. Over a period of six months the elder board, the pastor, and his associate led the church through some major structural changes. They consulted with Mark very little, yet the changes were going to affect his two areas of ministry the most. Mark felt they were unfair with him; their changes placed an undue amount of work onto an already loaded job description. Fortunately the annual church staff retreat came just at a critical moment. Mark was so offended by their unjust treatment of him that he had decided to leave. At the staff retreat, in the proper setting and with an adequate amount of time to work through the difficulties, the harmony of the team was spared. Mark decided to stay.

At another church retreat, the staff talked and prayed through a unified vision for a declining work. What had previously been a discouraged staff came back to the city determined to work to realize that vision.

A retreat is the best place and time for the fellowship "joints" of the growing body of Christ to vision. Paul suggests in Ephesians 4:15-16 that Christ must flow through those joints which connect us together if the body is to grow. Of course, the same is true with the staff. This is far more apt to happen as the team members find themselves in a new setting over an extended period, where genuine Christian relationships have the time necessary to function.

The Setting

Sociologists have written volumes on the effect our environment has on our minds and emotions. Thus it should come as no surprise when I suggest that an attractive and remote setting will establish the proper atmosphere for a dynamic staff retreat. Some teams have access to a cabin or cottage, which of course is ideal. Others have borrowed the facilities of a suburban or country church, while others have used a motel or retreat center. The key is to get far enough away so you won't be haunted by telephones, or by an urge to go home in the evening. The more rural and isolated, the better. If you have to cook your own meals, you'll profit by seeing each other in different servant roles. Plan to stay long enough to cover your agenda, but most of all, to allow the Spirit of God to blend your hearts into one. If you schedule more than one retreat a year, you may find staying over just one evening sufficient time. An annual event may need the greater part of three days and two nights to accomplish what needs to be done. Of course, the size of the team and the extent of the ministry will help determine how long the retreat should be.

A most unique staff retreat was written up in the Spring, 1981 *Leadership* magazine. The staff of Trinity Church in Seattle took a six-day stress camping adventure in the Sierra Nevada Mountains. It took many weeks of physical preparation before they were ready to go, but each one on the team testified to the enrichment of the experience. Different ones took turns leading the various days' excursions, which made everyone learn to yield to the leadership of other team members. They learned to struggle with their impatience, talk out their fears,, and learned to take risks with their own lives and with others on the team. The pastor said, "As we hiked, I kept having this sense we were like a miniature of the Christian church wandering through our own little wilderness. In some ways it would have been easier to go in eight different directions at eight different speeds. We were beginning to see that if we really loved each other, we had to accept one another's weaknesses and be sensitive to them. It was a matter of relinquishing our personal goals so the weakest member could regain strength and hope." Finally, he boasted that "a tested camaraderie had developed over six days of hiking in the wilderness, and we sensed it was here to stay."[2]

Their agenda wasn't written out or even anticipated, but I'm confident that there have been few experiences that have welded a team into a microcosm better than that one. They learned about Christian commitment by living on the trail, which is far more real that learning about it in a seminar in a comfortable setting. I like their theme verse from Psalm 61, "Lead me to the rock that is higher than I" (v. 2, KJV). Although I've not been on a staff trip like that, I've taken large groups of youth on the same kind of excursions, and I can testify to the oneness and growth that is developed among a group of people living under stress in God's beautiful outdoors. I'd recommend this kind of experience for any church staff.

The Working Agenda

This section is entitled "The Working Agenda" to emphasize that a team retreat is primarily for *working*. At times it will seem as if it's for fun, while other times when you're struggling through decisions and mending relationships, it may seem like torture.

If you're not taking a Sierra trek, you should plan a working agenda. If you don't, the tired ones and the loners will want to go off and hibernate. That's needed at times, too, but everyone must do it on cue at a planned retreat.

If you have agreed and practiced the guidelines in the chapter on the staff meeting, you will find the retreat to be very much like an extended staff meeting. One major difference will be the lengthy look at the past and the future. To build camaraderie, it is wise to have different people take the lead at different times. Intersperse free time and recreation among the study and planning sections so you will keep yourselves refreshed. Rather than having different people give devotionals, it would be wiser to have times of study when the whole team could interact with a portion of Scripture. Study passages on ministry, servanthood, the church, and other growth passages. Allow for extended prayer sessions throughout the day and seek to have an air of spontaneity and freshness.

Plan ample time for ministering to one another. Each person will have hurts, frustrations, concerns, and praises to share with the whole group. Each note of concern and praise should be integrated into rich times of prayer.

In planning the agenda which follows those personal times, keep three simple questions in mind as an overview for the business and planning sections. What do we do best? What do we need to improve? What ought we to do that we are not now doing?

I have noticed over the years that few staffs honestly evaluate their strengths. Because they don't, they fail to concentrate on them. They fail by default. I can't emphasize too much how important it is to examine carefully all the things you do well.

Just listen to what people say about your church. If they don't pass out many bouquets, then ask them what they think your church does best. Build on these strengths. There are too many churches in America who don't do anything well; they are known for nothing in particular, and consequently, attract very few people.

As you think about conducting new events and structuring new ministries, be sure they are an outgrowth of your church's philosophy and that now is the right time to inaugurate this particular new venture. To launch a new venture prematurely may mean an abortion rather than a birth.

The most helpful yearly planning retreats will include a time for each staff member to review his or her previous year's goal sheet, and in light of that, to share goals for the next year. These ought to include at least one's personal and ministry goals. Allow ample time to make the necessary changes so that all of these goals mesh with one another. Also allow time for certain goals to be challenged by other team members. Once you practice this every year, each team member will sense the built-in body pressure or accountability. It should prove a great motivating force to move the team along. If the team is functioning as it should, each member will endeavor to see that each suggested step of growth for the following year blends harmoniously with the rest of the team.

Let's say that the team's goal for the year is to get a much larger percentage of the body involved in ministry. The whole team will have a major function in getting this done. The pastor will be teaching and preaching a series of sermons on servanthood. The minister of Christian education will see that the human resource file is established and ready to function. The children's director, the minister of discipleship and evangelism, and the youth pastor will survey carefully their year's plans and determine what new personnel needs they have. Who is going to direct the training for all these people? What kind of promotion, finances, and personnel will it take to get the machine operating? A great deal of coordination will be needed to pull this off.

An excellent way to coordinate all of this work is to establish a work calendar indicating the various stages necessary to launch the events of the year. Show a line on the calendar for each event, with a date to indicate when each stage of the program is to be launched. Here is one example of the large calendar.

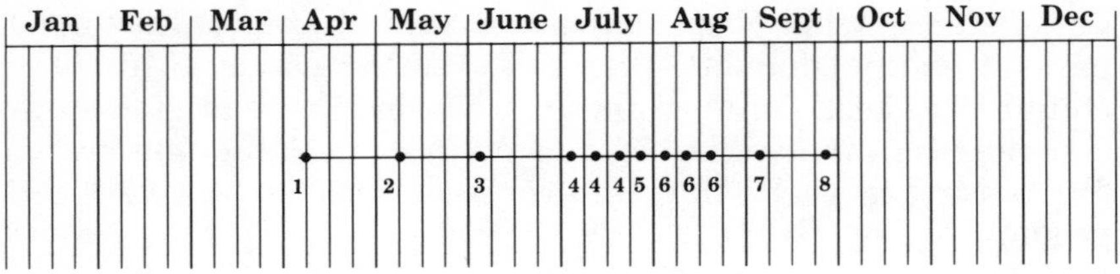

#1 Clearance with Christian Education Board
#2 Chairman of team appointed
#3 Team of people appointed to run programs
#4 Series of sermons preached on servanthood
#5 Notice in church newspaper about program and its purpose
#6 All youth and adult classes asked to complete form
#7 Mailing to people not completing form, including a cover letter
#8 Phone calls to people not completing form
Human Resource File completed

Start by placing a date on the calendar when the event is to be completed. Think backwards, asking yourself what steps it will take to see the final event culminated in an excellent fashion. Each week you will simply look at the appropriate section to learn what needs to be done on all the various programs. In this way, you need to be concerned only with that one phase of each project, and not load your mind with concern for all the other stages yet to come. Your mind will be at ease, with the knowledge that everything is being cared for. For each event, prepare a file folder with all the details to be tended to! Think through the details of each phase in advance and list them in the file.

Some calendars might list only an appropriate chronological number which refers to the corresponding page of details in the file. On a large calendar for the whole team, you can code the events with a color for each team member. It's conceivable that an active church might have as many as fifty events on the calendar. This provides a helpful way for everyone on the team to know what each member is currently engaged in. One of the strengths of this type of calendar is that it forces the low task-oriented person to become more organized. It will also help each one see how his or her activities fit into the total team plan. The problem of double scheduling of rooms or church vehicles should be avoided, and frantic last minute planning needs should not disrupt other needy events. Secretaries should know in advance what typing is to be done. The agenda for a meeting comes off this calendar, and the editor of the church newspaper can quickly check to see what items should be listed in the paper. It will force the pastor to give serious thought to his preaching schedule.

It shouldn't be hard to see that a major section of the retreat is needed for planning the calendar. Of course, this planning follows the discussion of next year's goals. It's also possible, of course, to add other things to the calendar as the year progresses. What a great way to start the year!

Project for Chapter 10

At the end of many of the chapters in this book, exercises are included which will facilitate the building of a godly microcosm. It would be helpful to evaluate and strengthen the cohesiveness of the team by working through one or more of those activities during your staff retreat. I would encourage you to work them on paper as prescribed. Allow ample time to gain the intended purpose of each project.

Part III: **Maintaining the Team**

11

HIRING NEW STAFF

"I **told** the search committee their background check didn't go back far enough."

11

HIRING NEW STAFF

FIFTY PERCENT of the people who go to church in America go to churches which have a multiple staff situation. This is a growing trend. Many have suggested that the day of the small congregation pastored by one person may be as foreign to American culture in the future as the small family business. A large majority of seminary graduates today leave their graduation lines and go to multiple-staff church positions. We as Americans are accustomed to specialization in every facet of our lives, and the church is no exception.

A great danger is inherent in this trend. I am in favor of hiring additional staff people. I have even established in the first chapter that it is a bona fide biblical concept. My concern is that many churches hire additonal staff at the wrong time in their church's history. They may have no need, or the motivation may be wrong.

When Not to Add New Staff

Following are some occasions when an additional staff person should *not* be hired. The candidate and the congregation should be aware of these red flags.

1. Unexplained Motives

Pastor Larry had just turned forty-five. During all of his years in the ministry, he had served as the sole staff member. In his current church, he seemed to have a hard time effectively ministering to the youth and the young married couples. Even though he was generally liked by the rest of the congregation, the members knew they needed to make a drastic move. Around the coffee cups one Sunday evening in an elder's home, it was decided that they suggest to their pastor that, since he was working so hard, he ought to have an assistant. They felt they either needed to do this or lose the younger part of their congregation. Pastor Larry was greatly honored by the suggestion. After all the routine procedures had been completed, a candidate was interviewed and hired. Joe's new job as minister to youth and young marrieds seemed to go well for him. In fact, it went so well that Pastor Larry became jealous of his new assistant. It caused a great deal of tension between them. What was once a minor problem now became a major one. Their team communication and cooperation dwindled to a dead standstill.

When Joe came for an interview, he was not able to detect the real motive behind the church's desire for an additional staff person. Who would tell?

Let this story be a warning to prospective candidates to dig deeper into the real cause for a church's hiring of additional staff. But also let this be a lesson to the congregation to be sensitive to their pastor's feelings and needs. There should be an honest and open communication about the hiring of additional staff. One church hired a youth pastor in hopes that this would stop their high school girls from getting pregnant! Of course, the youth pastor did not find this out until long after his arrival.

This story also teaches a second caution.

2. Inadequate Job Description

Be careful when the church hires its first assistant of any kind. This will likely be hard on the congregation, the pastor and, most of all, the newly hired person. The new situation is like that of an eighteen-year-old bride. She's excited about her new relationship, but, my oh my, there are so many things she never anticipated. The senior pastor didn't know what it would mean to share the affection of the congregation with another person. The associate may have anticipated a marvelous sharing of ministry, only to find himself struggling all alone without any counsel, or, at the other extreme, being ruled by a tyrant. The congregation thought it was going to be relieved of many tasks, only to find that now there was a broader ministry with additional work for them.

3. Unrealistic Expectations

A third caution naturally follows. Far too much may be expected of the new employee. This can lead to tension for him and frustration for the congregation and his fellow staff members. Herman Sweet warns us that:

> A young man just out of seminary with little experience and maturity may be expected to stretch himself effectively over a range of responsibility that has already proved too much for a mature, experienced pastor. He is expected to work with the church school,

> increasing its membership and attendance, improving parents' cooperation; he is expected to become the advisor for the youth groups so that the tired lay advisors can have a rest; he is expected to help with the calling and other pastoral duties; he is expected to be on hand at the church day and night so that he can be reached at any time.[1]

The list could go on and on. The poor chief of staff may not know how to protect the young man from all of this, or how to guide him into the proper role expectations. This only points out how important it is for all the parties concerned to be well prepared in advance for what is expected in their new relationship.

A pastor is normally considered to be a generalist, because of all the various and sundry things a pastor does throughout the course of his ministry. One caution in hiring a new staff person is not to hire another generalist, rather than a specialist. When this is done, the person may find himself being a "go-for," doing all the things the pastor doesn't want to do. Of more consequence is the fact that he has no specific ministry by which he can be evaluated or one in which he can find fulfillment. Numerous observant members of the congregation may find themselves asking, "What does Pastor Lawrence do anyway? I don't hear him preaching or leading any programs. What does he do with all his time?" It takes a very special personality with a high level of servanthood and a low drive for leadership and creative productivity to fill a role like that.

If a generalist is hired, he should be given some specific task (other than the items on the senior pastor's job description) such as business administrator or visitation minister. A contemporary trend that may prove effective is making the two men co-pastors. This takes a unique ability, especially on the part of the pastor who served as the leader prior to the new man's coming. This procedure tends to be more common in a congregation of three hundred or less. In such cases it is almost essential that both share the pulpit, because that is the way their being equal is most readily judged by the congregation.

Here is a list of generalist and specialist roles which could serve as a guide in making distinctions:

Doctrinally Ordered Professionals (Ordained)

Generalist

Pastors
Associate Pastors
Minister of Christian Education
Minister of Youth

Commissioned Professionals (Ordained or Unordained)

Specialist

Director of Christian Education or Youth Director
Director of Music or Minister of Music
Business Administrator
Specialized Ministries

Functionaries

Secretaries
Bookkeepers
Custodians

4. Ignoring Job Requirements

Usually during hard economic times there is a high rate of unemployment. When this is the case, a lot of people take positions because they need the money, even if they don't particularly have a strong desire to do that kind of work. Churches are known for their kindness, as they should be, but often fail to secure someone who has a great heart for ministry. In some cases, it would be better if the church gave the person a donation, rather than put him on the payroll.

5. Failure to Investigate

The last occasion is similar to the previous one, only it has a little different twist. It might be illustrated this way. Margaret and Chuck Moore had two teenagers in their church's youth group. Their nephew Jim had gone to Bible school for two years, but had dropped out because he couldn't make the grade. He had come for a visit during his summer vacation to Kansas where the Moores lived. In the course of the visit, he learned that the Moores' church was looking for a full-time youth pastor. The Moores were quick to inform the search committee that Jim would like to be considered for the position. The committee was impressed with his pleasing personality and with the fact that the Moores had given him such a fine recommendation.

When a church family is so deeply involved, as in this case, too little research is done on the candidate's experience, and few references checked. Even if they checked him out and found him lacking in skill and holiness, what could they do? The relatives would bring pressure to bear upon the search committee. Just because someone is at hand isn't a justifiable cause to put him on the staff. What makes it even worse is that the person is hired, and then found wanting. How in the world can he be released without upsetting the whole church?

Watch for these red flags.

When to Add New Staff

Many times in the history of a church, new staff ought to be added to the roster. Here are some key situations.

1. *The sheer numerical growth of the congregation often necessitates the hiring of new personnel.*

   Often the staff lacks time to minister to all the families who are joining the church. Back in the 60's the magic number was 250-300 members per staff person. Whenever that many more people were added to the congregation, it was time to add another staff member. In the 70's the number dropped to 175-200. In the 80's, churches are adding staff when there are 125-150 new members. The problem of national economics will certainly change this in many parts of the country in the 90's.

2. *No matter what the number or the new program might be, the true test is whether the hiring of new staff will enrich or deepen the ministry.*

   Herman Sweet suggests that "the purpose and the meaning of ministry is essentially no different for a staff of two, or five, or ten, than for a staff of one."[2] All that you have read about the strength of a team in the first chapter must be applied here. If a staff's task is mainly to equip the saints for ministry, then that should be the goal when new people are hired. If you want to add staff with the goal of having a flashier or more extensive program, rather than equipping people, then I question that you are ready to add to the staff. Never lose sight of the fact that the "saints are to do the work of the ministry," and the pastor-teachers are to equip them so they can better serve. Now, you may need more staff because the pastor needs more time to be free to study and pray in order that he can preach better. You may also need staff to carry on other equipping ministries such as music, discipleship, or evangelism.

3. *All of this leads us to consider the need for strengthening the ministry of different departments.*

   The children's department or the college department may soon become too large. A busy lay person may not have the time and energy to carry on all the administrative work of mobilizing participants and the necessary leaders. I see far too often a church who hires a youth pastor to minister to the youth, but he is too anxious to run with the gang, and the parents are too anxious to get rid of the task of being their chaperone and disciplinary marshall. No youth pastor is worth his salt who cannot recruit, train, and direct other adults (including the youths' parents) in an ever-expanding youth ministry. His task is ultimately to strengthen the ties between the youth and their families, not to divorce them from their families.

4. *Seldom does any one person have strengths in all four types of leadership capabilities.*

   In Chapter 4, where the four tasks of leadership were discussed, this was pointed out. The larger the congregation becomes, the more urgently a conceptualizing manager needs an operational manager. Seldom are these two leadership capabilities present in adequate quantities in the same person. The same is true with negotiating and promoting capabilities. A team needs all four capabilities in equal proportion, especially in a larger congregation where the amount of time needed cannot be supplied by laboring laymen. If these capabilities are lacking, there is an urgent need to hire additional staff. If this is the reason for hiring additional staff, then the staff members must function as a team, each utilizing his own strengths.

5. *The last reason for hiring new staff is lack of available lay people to do the work.*

   This is simply a sociological factor. For example, a trend that started during World War II is still with us and is constantly growing. The fact that there are more and more working mothers simply translates into the fact that there are fewer mothers to help do the ministry of Christian education in the churches. A frightening factor in 1982 was that only eight percent of Americans lived in what used to be called a normal family unit, that is, the original marriage for both husband and wife, with a non-working mother and at least one child under eighteen. I can't conceive of this trend ever turning around in America.

   Some people work long hours, or commute long distances, leaving little time for church activities. Some people live far from the church, making it difficult to give extra time. If the work of administrating education in most churches is ever to be accomplished, the church must pay to have it done.

Preparing the Church

In the average church, the addition of a staff person, or the replacement of any one staff member, will start a new chapter in the life of the church. Just as a marriage should not be hurried into, so a church should not rush into a new staff relationship. A wise, discerning young man who is courting a young woman does not rush into a proposal, even though he feels he is deeply in love. He is waiting to see how their relationship can stand the test of time and the pressure of various circumstances. Even then, when they marry, they both have some great surprises in learning who their mate really is. Courting any pastoral candidate is similar, only the problem is that the courtship usually lasts from two to ten days, and rather than one person making a choice, the whole congregation makes the choice and has to live with the new leader for who knows how long. This necessitates caution. A good, healthy match of pastor and parishioners is a divine act of God's grace.

I'm not sure there is a perfect way to go through the candidating process for either the church or their prospective leader, but here are some cautions.

1. The Law of Opposite Choice

Ted had a relatively wholesome marriage for twenty-seven years when his wife June was taken quickly in an automobile accident. He was not prepared to live alone. He went through all the grief stages before he even thought of marrying again. As he searched for a new wife, he thought this time it would be great to have a wife who was athletic. June was a good mother and wife. She was very domestic, but not very athletic. The children had been his athletic companionship, but now they were grown and away from home.

After a short but careful courtship with Margaret, they married. She loved to play tennis and swim and go to the athletic events in the community. It didn't take him long to miss the wonderful domestic traits that June had possessed. He had come to take them so much for granted that he didn't even consider looking for them in Margaret. This is so common it's almost a law. A man will often pick a second mate with opposite traits from his wife. Of course, this is even more true when the first marriage ended in divorce.

Numerous churches choose a new pastor with the same law in effect. The congregation will choose a person with skill and personality strengths that were lacking in the previous staff person. At times this is perfectly acceptable, because that's just what the congregation needs. Think through in advance what leadership strengths your church needs at this time. Do these match the strengths of the person selected?

Pastor Adams was an outstanding preacher. He was just what was needed to help Bethel Church get its first spurt of growth. He stayed for fifteen years and saw the church grow from fifty to five hundred members. The congregation adjusted to his impersonal style of indirect leadership. Of course, when Adams left Bethel, they called a warm, participative-style leader, who happened to be a mediocre preacher. Two hundred people left in the first year, even though they got what they wanted. If the congregation deliberately chooses an opposite, everyone ought to know what they are doing.

2. The Law of the Rushed Wedding

To avoid getting caught in the first problem, take adequate time in the interim. Herman Sweet suggests that a church ought to spend a year for the search. This may seem like a long time to many. It may be longer than needed, but it's better to be safe than sorry.

In some cases, churches need to go through all of the grief stages after the previous staff member leaves. Humans have a wonderful way of forgetting if enough time passes. But they grieve over the loss of a dearly beloved pastor. They grieve, but in a different way, over a pastor who divided the congregation or who was dismissed.

The congregation needs time to come to a common agreement over just what the church requires. Too many congregations keep switching from an associate to a minister of Christian education because they haven't taken the necessary time to think through what suits their needs best. They must search through all the resumes for just the right candidate, check all the references adequately, and think through what it will mean to share their affections with a new and different leader.

3. The Law of Interim Transition

Long pastorates are often the best. But many churches have died because their leader stayed too long. It takes the wisdom of Solomon to know when the pastor should pack his bags. I'm not suggesting that a man always leave when trouble comes. Sometimes it's wise to leave when the spiritual level of the congregation is at an all-time high. When a pastor leaves after he has had a long, successful pastorate, from twelve to fifty years, the congregation will face a painful transition to the next happy chapter in its history.

The man who follows this pastor may stay only a short time, because the members will have difficulty adjusting to a new style of leadership. This is due to the law of opposite choice. Their beloved leader's image must be washed out of their mind. It is especially healthy to plan on a long interim after a lengthy, successful pastorate. If the church doesn't, it is likely that the next pastor will serve only as an interim anyway. When he leaves, the congregation will have a depleted constituency and a lot of bitter feelings.

The major cause for the law of the interim transition is the tendency to compare. "We were accustomed to his great sermons, his warm, loving personality, his faithful calling, his constant attention to details, his strong leadership (or even his relaxed laissez-faire style of leadership)." Even the way the new leader makes the announcements or leads the communion service makes some people unhappy. They have grown too familiar with the way they used to do things. Thank the Lord there are enough mature people in the congregation who can make the adjustments, but too many people will have a hard time adjusting to new ways of doing things. Quiz the new leader thoroughly about his ability to implement change under these circumstances. He will need to be a master change agent.

4. The Law of Varied Expectations

This law has more to do with staff members, than with the pastor. Most American church people have common expectations about a pastor's role, but their expectations go in a thousand directions when it comes to an associate. One of the major steps of preparation for calling a new staff person is to adequately clarify for the candidate and the congregation what the ministry expectations are. Even though a staff person may be accountable to the pastor, his acceptance will vary in proportion to his success in meeting the expectations of each individual church member.

When John, the promising young graduate from seminary, arrived with his wife and baby daughter to replace a seasoned minister to the youth, everyone in the congregation had his or her checklist ready. The Joneses, whose son was going through a rebellious stage, were expecting John to bring their son back into fellowship with Christ. The sponsors were expecting many new ideas to help evangelize the high school. The elders were expecting John to attract the kids who were on the periphery of the group. They expected that many new families would join the church because John was there. The pastor expected that through John's discipleship ministry many of their youth would go to Bible college and enter the ministry. Some expected him to entertain the group. Others wanted him to lead on missionary trips, and yet others expected a new thrust in the group's musical endeavors. You can readily see that the list could go on and on. Poor John is caught in the squeeze unless some well thought-out guidelines and role expectations are provided for him to follow and for the congregation and its leaders to use as an evaluation tool.

Mary graduated from seminary and moved to California to marry. She and her husband joined Trinity Church while her husband was finishing graduate school. Mary worked in the educational program before she was hired to become the children's worker. It was simply announced in the church newspaper one Sunday that Mary would take on her role as children's worker the first of March. There was no discussion with the lay educational workers. They were not even asked if they wanted someone to help, nor were they told what their working relationship with her would be. Some departmental workers resented her trying to show leadership in what was their domain. Her ministry was greatly limited for the first year, and it was only because of her gracious, serving spirit that she became effective later. Proper preparations with the congregation could have greatly enhanced her ministry.

Even though there are many problems with the use of job descriptions, when they are properly written and used, they can keep people like John and Mary from ministry suicide. The congregation needs to have clearly explained to them verbally and in writing what the new staff person is expected to accomplish, both in his early and later years of service, and what his working relationship will be to others.

5. The Law of Changed Roles

Every new staff member who joins the team changes the complexion of the group dynamics so much that the job descriptions change for the other staff members. Unless the congregation and the team are prepared for this, it could develop disappointments among the congregation and within the team.

Jerry Anderson, who carried the title of Associate Minister of Christian Education, was the second man on the staff of the growing First Church. After much discussion and searching, Richard joined the team as Minister to Youth. Richard was to supervise the adult and children's departments, plus supervise the visitation and evangelism work of the church. Jerry's job description was changed, because he no longer had to work with the youth, as he had done before. The senior pastor's job description was also changed, because he was no longer responsible for guiding the church's visitation program. Jerry found it difficult when the youth program took a different direction, and many parents and their children still came to him for counsel about their family problems. It's important to talk to the whole congregation and prepare them for upcoming changes.

The Search Committee

Each church's constitution will determine how the search committee, or calling committee, will be formed. If possible, the committee should be chosen from various age groups and organizations within the church family. The committee considering the calling of a minister of children's work, for instance, should be comprised of parents, a representative of the church's committee of Christian education, the official church board, a representative from the various clubs and organizations that the person will supervise, plus a representative from the pastoral staff. Often the committee will include a representative at large from the congregation.

Here are some simple guidelines to keep in mind.

1. Gather resumes from as many sources as possible.
2. Be sure you have gathered all the information about role expectations before you go about selecting your candidate.
3. Make a thorough inquiry as to the candidate's experience and character from numerous references.

   Keep in mind that all of his references will give you favorable comments. Therefore it is wise to ask those giving the references for names of additional people who know the candidate. Phone calls are often better sources of information than written references. Certain kinds of people give more accurate references than others. A person who has worked with the candidate can give you a much more complete reading than the person's pastor, his friends, or one of his teachers. People cannot give you a good understanding of how a candidate works with others unless they themselves have observed him at work. Often I've given a glowing recommendation for a student who performed like a true scholar in the classroom, only to find to my embarrassment that he couldn't get along with people in a working situation.

You might ask the candidate's permission to run a credit check and consider requesting medical and psychological assessments. Find out about his spiritual example, marriage, family, preaching and teaching, his study and devotional habits, and his doctrinal position. Don't be afraid of being too thorough. (The next chapter gives more details about the interview.)

I've seen many churches take only their first impression of a person, or the candidate's own answers about himself, as sufficient information to qualify him as their selected candidate. Many of those situations turned out to be a disaster. Check out a person thoroughly before asking him or her to be on your staff.

Fred Smith stated in an article in *Leadership* magazine: "A law firm once told me that they paid almost no attention to references anymore; they could learn everything they wanted to know by studying the person's history instead. Their belief was that successful people will be successful in the future, and failures will be failures. They also found that most failures are very adept at explaining their failures, and when you start buying stories, you are only presenting an opportunity to fail once again. Research shows that in 90% of cases the future behavior and performance of a leader will be an extension of his past." Keep in mind that this is a business approach. Perhaps the person has not yet found God's niche for him.

4. Continually ask the congregation to join you in prayer for wisdom in all your deliberations. I would strongly recommend that you study Friesen's book, *Decision Making and the Will of God*, in preparation for this major undertaking. Check your theology about God's will against Friesen's very thorough dissertation on the subject of the call to ministry.
5. Send a thorough job description and a complete profile of the church and its community to the candidates.
6. Keep all the candidates informed about your progress and where they stand in your deliberations.
7. Narrow your selection down to your first preferences.
8. Make sure the senior pastor is agreed with your final selection before you go to the congregation for ratification.
9. Give the congregation a regular up-to-date summary

without the listing of any names. (That could be an embarrassment to the candidates if the information were known outside the committee.)

10. Only present one candidate to the congregation at a time. Put all of the pertinent information about that candidate in writing and circulate it among the congregation prior to his coming.
11. Make sure the candidate has, long before he arrives, a thorough schedule and outline of his responsibilities during the candidating period.
12. Pay for the travel expenses of the candidate and his wife (and perhaps his family) to come for your interview.
13. Give all of the congregation a chance to hear the candidate speak and to ask all the questions they want answered.
14. Make sure that before the vote is taken everyone knows what percentage of the vote is necessary to extend the call.
15. Have a secret ballot. Give consideration to having a place for comments on the ballot. A "no" vote often is not a vote against the candidate, but rather against some other factor, such as the position, the lack of money, the wrong conditions of the call, or even the wrong job title. When the candidate makes his decision to accept or reject the call, he ought to know what the negative votes meant.
16. Put the conditions of the call in writing to the candidate before you expect him to make a final decision.
17. Inform all the other candidates and organizations with whom you have been corresponding about the fact that the position has been filled.

Searching for Candidates

In the 80's major changes have occurred in the resources used to fill staff positions. The surprising thing is that it hasn't come about because of the lack of worthy, capable seminary and Bible school graduates. In fact, at no time in the history of the American church has there been more trained clergy. A great deal of the change has to do with a new mind-set in the church. People who are trained in parallel professions and who have served the church faithfully are many times chosen over inexperienced people who have a three or four-year seminary degree. Experienced people are known quantities. They are tried and proven. A man with a business degree or a teaching certificate who has grown up in the church and has been faithful in his personal walk with the Lord and in the church may be the church's first choice for their new minister of Christian education. The pastor's attitude may be, "We know just what we're getting."

Joan had worked in a Michigan suburban church in the children's department for many years while her children were growing up. The nest was empty now and her husband had done very well in his own business. When their church was looking for a children's worker, they hired Joan for a salary much lower than any other candidate would have needed. She started out with a ten-year advantage over other candidates because of her experience in working in the children's department.

An Oregon church hired three one-dollar-a-year men who each gave one day a week to their respective assignments. They could do this because they were self-employed or in a profession where they could take a day a week for such a new task. One man was the minister of Christian education, another the minister of discipleship and evangelism, and the third was the church's business manager. Of course, they also gave some time on their weekends. The church hired one secretary to handle many of their details during the week. Each man had an office and a phone. The church got the involvement of four new staff people and their families for the price of a part-time secretary. These men were already deeply involved in the church and had the many acquaintances necessary for recruitment and team work. It was important that they were given titles and positions, because that gave them the necessary prestige for respected leadership.

A third new source of leadership is the church family. They are people who retire, some early, to take part-time ministries in their churches. They take positions such as business managers in the church or visitation pastors. Frank Tillapaugh in his book, *The Church Unleashed*, talks about how his church, Bear Valley Baptist Church, encourages people in their congregation to give themselves full-time to a ministry that God has especially laid on their hearts. The church mission's budget helped to finance this new work. The church has a diverse and exciting outreach ministry because its people are truly released to minister to their congregation and their community.

Of course, there are many formal and traditional ways to find very well-qualified personnel. Evangelical seminaries are equipping people for ministries in greater numbers than ever before. They tend to be older and often more mature because they are often second-career people. In 1982 the average age of

American seminarians was 32. The best way to contact these seminary students is to talk to the placement office of the seminary that reflects your doctrinal bent. Denominational headquarters — both state, district, and national — have a service available to help you in securing resumes. Some headquarters are using computer printouts to help match your church with a person who best meets your needs. They work on the same basis as a dating service for singles.

Another source to look to for help is especially useful for small churches. You may call it a shared ministry. Churches today are sharing secondary staff people the way rural churches have shared itinerant pastors for years. This is especially true of ministers of Christian education, and college and high school directors. Another version of this is the cooperative venture with parachurch organizations. An organization such as Word of Life can greatly aid your church's youth work by training your youth sponsors even though they may come only once a month or so to your church building. Some large churches who give birth to a small congregation share their staff with the new congregation for training and service.

A small church which feels it cannot have an additional staff person perhaps now will utilize these additional ways to secure people power. With the many changes in American working structures, we can expect to see a stronger shift to creative ministries in the 80's and 90's.

Project for Chapter 11

A Pastor's Priorities

What are the priorities on the minister's time in your congregation? What does the minister see as the order of priority on his time? What do the members believe it to be?

One way to find the answers to these and related questions in your parish is to use a set of cards similar to those shown here.

Visiting	*Teaching*
Calling in the homes of members or at their place of work in a systematic program to meet each member on his/her own turf.	Teaching the instruction class, planning and/or teaching classes for church school teachers, teaching in special short-term classes, etc.

Leading Worship and Preaching
Planning and conducting worship services, including sermon preparation and working with others who will participate in leading corporate worship.

Enabler
Helping others identify their own special call to service and ministry and enabling them to respond to that call.

Evangelism
Calling on the unchurched people in the community, bearing witness to the Good News, calling on prospective new members, and training laymen to be evangelists.

Counseling
Counseling with individuals on personal and spiritual problems, with couples planning to be married, with those who are hospitalized, with people who have personal and vocational problems, etc.

Administration
Serving as "executive secretary" of the congregation, working with committees, helping to plan the financial program of the church, working with committees on planning and implementing programs, etc.

A Leader Among Leaders
Serving with the lay leadership as one of the core of leaders in the congregation —each with his/her own special responsibilities and each with his/her own unique gifts.

Community Leader
Serving as a volunteer leader in the community to help make this a better world for all God's children.

The Leader
Serving as the leader in the congregation—the person to whom members turn for advice and guidance on all aspects of the life and work of the congregation.

Personal and Spiritual Growth
Developing and following a discipline of Bible and other devotional study, participating in programs of continuing education, and helping to plan and lead opportunities for personal and spiritual growth for others.

Denominational Responsibilities
Carrying a fair share of denominational responsibilities, participating in other cooperative bodies. Also enlisting denominational and other resources for use in the local situation.

1. Reproduce enough copies so each member of the committee will have one set listing the priorities for the pastor's time.
2. Call together six to eight leaders in your congregation, such as the people who served on the pulpit committee when the present pastor was called, or on the pastor/parish relations committee or its equivalent.
3. Cut the sheet so each person has one set of cards; distribute these packs of cards to the people around a table.
4. Clarify the ground rules. Is the question "What *are* the priorities on the pastor's time in this congregation?" or "What *should* be the priorities?" or something else? Make sure everyone is responding to the same question.
5. Give everyone from five to ten minutes to look at the cards and sort them out, discarding what he believes to be the four *lowest* priorities on the pastor's time or the least important functions. *Without discussing what they are doing or the reasons for their choices*, each person should arrange the remaining cards in the order of importance.
6. Begin with one of the laymen and, moving in rotation around the table, ask each person to lay down his top priority card, face up on the table. While doing this, let each person state what he has chosen as the top priority and why. Continue around the table until everyone has placed his top priority card on the table. (It is often helpful if the minister is the last to show his card.)
7. Discuss what the cards reveal. Are they all the same? Are there differences? If so, what do the differences suggest?
8. Continue the same pattern, with each person laying his second priority card just below the one placed on the table earlier. Discuss what the trend appears to be.
9. Continue with six more rounds.
10. Look at the four cards each person discarded earlier. Is there anything resembling a consensus in the discards?

Use this in any way you wish as a tool to stimulate creative and constructive discussion. Have fun!

(Adapted and used by permission of Lyle Schaller)

Part III: **Maintaining the Team**

12

CONDUCTING THE INTERVIEW

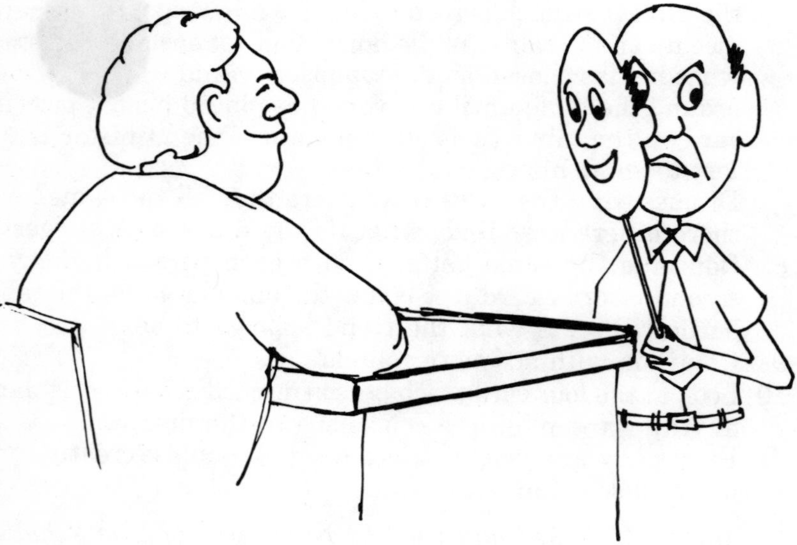

"Oh, yes, I'd be glad to do that."

12

CONDUCTING THE INTERVIEW

NO PART OF the candidating process could be considered unimportant, but none could be considered more important than the interview. Most persons are masters at the art of giving great first impressions. It takes a skilled individual or committee to see through the facade to the real person. Because it is difficult even for a trained personnel secretary to do this, businesses are currently trying new techniques, such as a dual interview. A second person is seated behind a one-way glass observing the candidate. He gets only the body language impressions. When the interview is completed, the audio and visual parts of the interview are compared. If there is any discrepancy between the two, the visual is given more credibility because that states more honestly the real person. I'm not suggesting that you go to such lengths to get a genuine picture of the candidate, but what follows can be a great help in opening the windows of the soul of the candidate so you have a better idea of who the person is.

This chapter is based on the presupposition that you want to hire the most capable person possible for your staff position. Small congregations think that they cannot afford a highly qualified person. After all, they are just a small church. However, if you have only two people on the staff, and one of them is a mediocre leader, then fifty percent of your staff is inferior. Small churches tend to think second-rate because of their size. Too often they are like a young man with a poor self-image who will take just any woman because he thinks he doesn't deserve anyone better. So the church's self-image tends to be reflected by the quality of persons it secures.

Here are some simple things to consider when you interview. Although many of these items apply to both the candidate and the interviewing committee, you will find a list of guidelines for each.

Guidelines for the Search Committee

Listen carefully for the flow of communication. It can be a big indicator of the candidate's communication skills. Watch not just for the substance of the answers given, which of course is critical, but also for the person's ability to dialogue. This can be a major factor in letting you know his capability at personal relationships. Does he answer your questions directly? Does he interrupt the one who is speaking, or does he give the person speaking his undivided attention? Does he stay with the subject at hand or tend to jump subjects? Does he ask questions, as well as answer them? Does he reflect a tense manner, or is he relaxed with people in difficult settings?

If he does not have some searching and provocative questions, then you ought to doubt his ability to handle the job. I would be complimented by questions which I hadn't thought through myself. If he asks only fill-in-the-blank type of questions, I would doubt his mental capabilities to think clearly through the issues involved with the ministry. I would hope he would want to know more than what day he could have off, and who was his boss. I would be far more impressed with qualifying questions about why we have structured our adult ministries this way and not in another fashion.

Second, avoid a list of questions on a worksheet. These tend to make the interview stilted and formal. Consequently, this book will not give that type of list, but instead will give categories of things to look for and general ways of getting at the true answers. Another reason for staying away from a list is that candidates are like students in a classroom who know how to give the answer the teacher expects. Consequently, it is far more important to phrase your questions in the form of short case studies or illustrations rather than as direct questions. It's easy to ask such questions as, "Are you in favor of staff meetings, do you like to design your own programs, are you as a pastor in favor of discipleship, do you respond to authority?" Most people will respond favorably to this type of question, but do they in fact practice such things? No person would admit that he does not obey authority, but a person rebelling against authority in certain situations, may not realize he is. A good interviewer will find out when such situations occur. So it's much better to give a situation where the candidate would have to respond to authority, and then ask him how he would handle it. Ask the person what format he has followed in his private worship during the last month, rather than asking if he has private worship.

Keep thinking of ways your requirements for the position will be expressed in the actual ministry process.

A third idea is that the interviewer will rephrase the candidate's comments for clarification and interpretation. Verbalize back to him or her, "This is what I hear you saying" kind of messages—"John, you say you enjoy doing door-to-door visitation. Is that right?"

"Oh, yes. I've done a great deal of that."

"Does that mean that we can expect you to be engaged in it about seven hours a week?"

"Yes, I think that's right."

"Great. How many calls did you average during the last month at the church where you are now employed?"

You are not doing this because you cannot trust him. You want to be sure you get a clear picture of exactly what he means.

When you are trying to get a person to be transparent and open with you, the best way to do this is by initiating that same process yourself. It's amazing how your openness tends to open others. As a committee member, you can tell the candidate about the struggles the church has had, or about your desire to develop rapport with a certain group, or your personal struggle to try to spend sufficient time with your family.

Before the interview, each committee member should have a copy of all the material pertaining to your candidate. Note the items you need to *clarify* from the resumes and references. Make sure sufficient attention is given to the job description. Rather than asking if he agrees to work with the parents of the youth, ask him for illustrations about the way he sees this actually being worked out.

Every candidate for any job should have multiple interviews. This is especially important if he or she will be working with a team. As time permits, plan interviews with each team member separately, but definitely plan an interview with the team as a whole. The major task with the group is to determine the feasibility of his working with the team. Every candidate ought to spend the most time with the chief of staff, but the chief of staff should not delude himself by thinking he can get the complete reading alone. Because of various perceptual mechanisms, each team member will see a different facet of the candidate's personality and capabilities.

Fred Smith of Dallas who has hired numerous people says, "The hiring person should be the customer, not the salesman. I refuse to hire a person who does not say something along the way that makes me hire him. I assume this person will not make it, until I am convinced otherwise. When it comes to hiring, I am not trying to be benevolent; I am on a search for outstanding qualities."

Qualities to Look For

A man in charge of hiring in a large Nazarene church made a surprising statement. He said he wasn't so much concerned about what the person knew about the job to be done, or the experience he had. He said that as long as the person was teachable, and was characterized by a holy character and a high energy level, he could make him into a productive staff person. I've seen this in secular corporations as well. I'd like to rearrange and expand his list of qualities, and then add some insight on each point. You should be more concerned about the total person rather than just his ability to perform a certain task or show a certain level of love.

1. Commitment Level

A leading industrial firm was hiring a new man for a middle management position. Each applicant in the interview was asked what he would like to be. The man who was finally hired said that he wanted to be president of that firm. It was a characteristic of his commitment level. The Bible pictures an elder as one who is worthy to be hired because he works. The elder isn't looking out for his own skin. He is a goal-oriented person who sees the challenge of his ministry as being far more important than the benefits this ministry position can bring him. The candidate should be concerned about his family's well-being, but if questions say more about how much time he can spend with his family, how many nights he can expect to be at home, and how many office hours he needs to put in each day, rather than the challenge of his task, then I'd question his commitment level. The person's weight may tell you about his energy level. You ought to be far more concerned with the candidate's productivity than with the hours he or she spends on the job.

Questions that deal with how much time a person spends preparing sermons should weigh as much as how many tasks he can accomplish in a week. Questions that reveal his creativity are also helpful. A committed person sees tasks to be done before being told. For more insight, check with people who have worked with the candidate in the past. What a person does with his spare moments gives you an understanding of his energy level. If he exercises, and has the discipline to do it by himself even when he doesn't feel like it, you get a clue that he is ambitious. An ambitious person will begin work without being told, and will do it even when he doesn't feel well. He will learn how to go around the detours which seem to block his success, and he will be thinking about the next task before the present one is finished.

2. Godliness

Commitment that is not wrapped in godliness may be worse than a godly person without commitment, because the labor will be in vain. The psalmist warns us that "unless the Lord builds the church we labor in vain that build it." This implies that we can build the church in our own strength. That ought to frighten us a great deal.

Many attempts have been made to design an instrument that would test godliness. Stop looking for such a device, because no one has ever designed this instrument. Dr. Vernon Grounds has a simple test to gauge one's own personal holiness. He suggests that you should do a noble task which costs you greatly. Determine that you will never tell a soul after you have done it. When it is finished, see how desperately you want to tell someone. That will tell you what your motives were to begin with.

Even though we are unable to test the quality of a person's godliness, certain clues might be a barometer to give us a reading. The Pioneer Ministries of British Columbia discovered after years of employing hundreds of people that those who have the most pious air in interviews and on resumes often are the least godly. I've noticed this same thing myself. Keep this in mind when looking for clues to a person's godliness.

I would rather know what particular trait of holiness the person is asking the Lord for currently, than if he prays. I would rather know when was the last time he gave an evangelistic testimony to someone, than if he feels that he has the gift of evangelism. When was the last time he had to ask for forgiveness is a better clue than if he feels he is humble.

The first time I met Senator Mark Hatfield in Oregon, when he was still Secretary of State, he asked me what I had received from God's Word that day. This kind of question is better than, "Do you regularly read the Bible?"

"What are you currently doing to resolve bad feelings you have toward a fellow Christian?" may seem like an intrusive question, but I'd be more pleased with an embarrassed answer about such a struggle than with a statement that he has none. These are some windows to your candidate's spiritual pilgrimage that will tell you how well he will fit into your microcosmic staff.

3. Character

You can only truly understand a person's character by looking at a combination of his personality and his ethics or values. It's almost as hard to get a handle on this as it is to comprehend a person's spiritual depth. You may never get a true picture of his character until he finds himself in a difficult or stressful situation. The Lord suggested that the saints would go through a testing of their faith which would prove the quality of their faith. Questions about how he handled situations in his past, or how he would face certain situations in the future, might give you insight into the depth of his character. It is critical to have an accurate reading on this because those stressful moments will come, and they can rend a team and even a church apart, if there is no genuine godly character built into the very fiber of the soul. The church is a place for building character, and at times even a staff person will find this kind of testing. The concern here is not that the person be without faults, but that he know how to properly handle the stressful moments when they come.

Stories which set up situations where a person's genuine character will be revealed are the kind of cases you would like your candidate to interact with. They will have to do with loyalty, honesty, forgiveness, acceptance, and so on. Perhaps the best study of godly character in the Bible is to be found in 1 Timothy 3:1-13, where the spiritual qualifications of an elder are given. I agree with the scholars who believe that the first one, "above reproach," is the overview of all the rest listed in that passage. Some people are using the "Spiritual Leadership Quotient Inventory," written by Frank Wichem of Believer Renewal Resources, as an instrument to test a person's character.

An important aspect of a person's character is his personality. You will want a person who can laugh at himself, and who doesn't hold a grudge, but instead depicts 1 Corinthians 13 style of love. You will also want to check out his self-image. Can you distinguish in his character the fine line between ego strength and pride? People will soon be turned off by pride, but will follow a leader whose ego strength is clothed with a meekness shown by his dependence upon God. People want someone who knows where he is going and has a pretty good idea of how he's going to get there. Just ask a person to talk about who he is, what he has done, and how he has done it, and you will soon discover what his motivation is. Is it pride, ego strength, or does he have such a low self-esteem that he couldn't lead anyone anywhere? Take a good look at Paul's description of ego strength in Romans 12:3, "Do not think of yourself more highly than you ought, but rather think of yourself with sober judgment, in accordance with the measure of faith God has given you" (NIV). Do you see in him a sense of pride, or a sense of "I can do all things through Christ who strengthens me?"

You want to hire a person who is teachable. If he is going to be a team person and fit in with your church's philosophy of ministry, then he must be willing to bend with the consensus of the team. A genuinely intelligent person will show his wisdom at this point. He knows what to die for and when to flex with the team. It is meaningless to ask a person if he is flexible. Of course, everyone thinks he is. You may get genuine insight from others he has worked with in the past. Have the candidate tell you how he worked through a compromise with others in the past year. The true test of compromise is shown only when he had to give in to their program, their idea, or on some issue that he considered to be of vital importance to him personally.

No doubt you can find out most about a man through his wife. Many leading corporations feel they can find out more about a man by interviewing his wife than by interviewing the man himself. Do not be deceived into thinking that you are only hiring a man, and not his wife. You may only be paying the man, but he is influenced by his wife. Besides, no one knows him better. The way he acts at home is a far greater insight into his character than how he acts in a church meeting. What special attention and honor he gives his wife, and the way he treats the children, will let you know how flexible and loving he really is. You will want to know a lot about how he acts at home if you want to truly know him. What is the decision making process at home? I would want to know from the wife what she sees as her husband's strengths and weaknesses. Is he orderly, and how does he do with the family finances? In your conversations with the candidate's wife, however, don't put her on the spot or embarrass her. Treat her as a partner.

One of the most significant things about a man's personality is his love for people. For example he cannot hide behind the fact that he is a task-oriented person; this only means that he has to work all the more on loving others. You will want to know what special acts of love your candidate has shown during the past six months.

If a church staff is to model to the congregation how people who are truly godly interact with one another, you need people who have the signs of godly character. Not that they are perfect, but they should demonstrate that they all live within God's redemptive context where there is giving, sharing, forgiving, and loving of one another. A church's staff cannot be a place for immature people. It cannot be a halfway house for those who someday will grow up.

4. Ministry Skills

You may have put this first on your list. I have put it toward the end, because being a skilled worker is of little value in God's work unless there are strengths in the other areas already mentioned.

It's important to have a clear-cut job description before you can evaluate a candidate's ministry skills. You will soon find out if you have an adequate job description when you start to evaluate how it's going to be fulfilled.

Sometimes people who are qualified for a special ministry are turned down for that position merely because they don't know how to answer questions about special ministries. Jim was being interviewed for a position as minister of discipleship and evangelism. When he was asked how he would develop these ministries, he answered just as he was taught in school. "Well, I'd study the neighborhood, the congregation, find out who was available and willing to help, then I'd design a ministry to meet the needs in my area of ministry." Now, that's not an uneducated answer, but to some people it would look as if he didn't know what he would do. Many committee members haven't worked through a good evaluation process before deciding goals and strategies. They simply think about programs. If a candidate doesn't have six good programs to plug into any given situation, then they think he isn't qualified. Jim's answer was good as far as it went, and would have been satisfactory for some people. The interviewer should ask Jim to give specifics. And Jim should be able to read his interviewers. He should elaborate upon his answer by saying that he could see one of the six programs he has worked with in the past possibly fitting into their church. Then he should have some specific suggestions to offer.

You will want to discern signs of a candidate's ability to delegate, to organize, to recruit, to be a goal setter and implementer, and to be creative. You will want to know what books he has read recently in his field of endeavor. What are the latest concepts in his field that he has most recently thought through?

It would be fitting to speak of the importance of experience here. Too many committees see this as the paragon of all qualifications. The problem is that it could have been years of poor experience. A wise committee will see that it may be more important to find a brilliant, promising, teachable, and energetic candidate, than to have a person who has served twelve years and done a fair job, but who wasn't an outstanding leader.

Pastoral Style of Leadership

A person's predominant style of leadership is significant. A good leader will know how and when to switch his styles, but each leader tends to favor one particular style. The way you mark a candidate on the following graph will give you a good reading on his style of leadership. Each one of the seven factors in the left-hand column influences a person's style.

FINDING THE BEST STAFF TEAM MEMBER

Pastoral Style of Leadership				
Factors which affect the leader's style	*Laissez-Faire* (observe, not control the individual)	Democratic Participative (full-team)	Autocratic Delegator (partial-team)	Benevolent Autocratic (controlled individual)
	← no control			total control →
1. Temperament style	Negotiating manager	Operational manager		Conceptual and promotional manager
2. Personality makeup	Laid back Non-aggressive personality	Enjoys being with people, yet a certain level of task orientation	Has conception of where he's going, yet seeks to get others to join him	Type A leader Super aggressive and demanding
3. Denominational background	Tendencies toward liberal view of theology	Middle of the road Evangelical		Tendencies toward Fundamentalism
4. Past and present educational input	Concern for process theology	Looks for balance of content and process	Authoritative philosophy of education	Strong concern for theological content and life-style absolutes
5. The church's financial control	The pastor could care less about the finances	Pastor, board, and congregation make decisions together	Pastor directs the board's decisions on finances	Pastor controls
6. Age and longevity of this ministry	May be in first chapter of his stay	(May not affect either)		Pastor may have started church has long tenure
7. Family constellation	Middle child	Last child		Firstborn and only child

Ask the candidate for information on each one of the seven points and to seek to determine where on the chart he would score on the various items. This chart is of great value for either a committee looking at a candidate, or for a new staff member looking at the prospects of working with another pastor. This will give him a clue about how well his style of leadership will mesh with the resident pastor and his staff. Even though your philosophy of ministry may be alike, that does not guarantee that you can work together. You need to be just as concerned about your style of leadership and control as you are about your philosophy.

1. Temperament Style — The temperament style is explained in depth in Chapter 4. You may see the candidate's style so influenced by other factors that you may choose to place his dominant characteristics in other columns.

2. Personality Makeup — See the section on personality in this chapter. You will be looking mainly for the desire to control or lead. Keep in mind that no one is right and the others wrong. Each type has its own strengths. This study will help you know what you can expect of the candidate later.

3. Denominational Background — Many people have had numerous church affiliations in our mobile society. Yet one tends to be a dominant one. Because fundamentalists stress more theological and life-style absolutes, these people seek to be on the controlling side.

4. Past and Present Educational Input — If a person did his undergraduate work at a fundamentalistic school and he is now working on an advanced degree in a state school or one that leans more toward liberal theology, this may indicate a shift in his thinking. Because of the personality of an individual, you may see him moving one way or another on the graph. An evangelical is more apt than others to be in any one of the four squares.

5. The Church's Financial Control — You need to be concerned here with what the candidate sees as the ideal, and the way he dealt with the finances in the previous churches where he worked.

6. Age and Longevity — This is an item which may have no bearing on your interviewing process. It should be an item of concern for a staff person if he is considering the prospect of working with another pastor. A beloved pastor may be basically a no-control style leader, but just because he's been there for so many years, he may have some deep ruts set in his pattern of leadership. You will surely want to know how open he will be to someone else's ideas.

7. Family Constellation — Psychologists have written books about the family birth order. Their research tells them that the place in which you were born in the line of children in your family will affect the way you play out your marriage role and your leadership role in your vocation. Be aware of exceptions to these rules before putting too much stock in this factor. For instance, you may be the third child born, but because there were eight years between you and the previous child, you no doubt were raised as a last child. Lyle Schaller makes extensive reference to this point in his book, *Multiple Staff in the Larger Church.*

Although you may not choose to make an acid test of this point, my observations are that an obvious firstborn who is a take-control type leader may find it hard to work under a last-born *laissez-faire* senior pastor. There are many greatly frustrated associates who work with men like that. It can be done, but it takes a lot more effort on the part of both persons.

8. Team Person — If you are really seeking to develop a microcosmic team, this point is significant. What makes this hard to discover is that sometimes a staff member worked in beautiful harmony with one person or team, but may miserably fail with another person or group. Many of the previous points on this chart will give some clues about your compatability. Above all, don't simply ask either the candidate or his references if he works well with a team. Most people work reasonably well on a team. Ask for specific examples of how he relates to other team members.

Other checkpoints include the candidate's willingness to submit to authority. At the same time, you don't want a yes-man. I have made a couple of long-lasting friends while serving with them on boards. I have gained respect for them just because they weren't yes-men. We would carry on a heavy dialogue in the meetings, even to the point of calling it an argument. We all knew that we wanted the best solution. We would argue until someone proved his point. Those are team men, not rubber stamps. They make a team profitable because they iron out the best solution through their dialogue. When you're interviewing a candidate, try to find out how he solves problems in a group.

Keep in mind that you are apt to gain some of the greatest insight into who a candidate is as the days of the candidating process move along. Watch how comfortable he is when he meets strangers. Observe how he respects property. See when and how often he initiates spiritual matters into the conversations. Is he courteous in his driving and with strangers?

After you have covered all the major items of concern, you will want to talk about the finances. If the candidate starts out asking what his benefits are, you may have a clue about where his values are. The next chapter deals with the financial package and how to make that an ethical and courteous consideration in the call.

Guidelines for Candidating

When Frank came back from the Navy, he went to Sylvia's home to meet his prospective in-laws. They were not at home, so he went into a bedroom off the living room to get into his civvies. He was, of course, nervous about the special meeting. When he came into the living room, the family had arrived and were waiting to meet him. They went into utter shock when they saw him. He was so nervous that he had forgotten to put on his pants.

Being interviewed for a desired position can be as nerve-wracking, and may cause you to make equally stupid mistakes. To take the pressure off, here are some guidelines. Keep in mind many of the points in the previous chapter on the candidating process, but these items are of special interest to you. If you are overly anxious for the job, you may forget to ask a critical question.

1. The most important thing is to know who the people are you will be working with, and how you see your personalities and skills meshing. Use the chart on page 172 to study the seven characteristics of the staff's leadership style.
2. Does the staff work as a team, or are they like married singles, each working totally alone?
3. Gain understanding in great detail about what would be expected of you. Ask questions colored by live examples to gain the fullest amount of clarification about the church's expectations.
4. Go over your job description carefully to be sure you understand everything.

5. Check carefully all church documents, such as the constitution and bylaws. Ask questions about anything that you feel needs further clarification.
6. Get all the information you can about the church's past and present history. Were there any splits in the past? Why, and what was the outcome? What is the leadership potential currently? What is the commitment of the congregation to the church's ministry? Why is the church growing, or declining? How many adult converts have there been in recent months? Who is doing the evangelism (other than the pastor)?
7. Get as complete a neighborhood profile as is possible. What is the median age? Is it a changing neighborhood? Is the church's median income greater than the neighborhoods? If so, this may be a strong clue that the church will have a hard time sociologically integrating its neighborhood converts into the congregation.
8. Who was the last person who held the position for which you are being interviewed? How well was he received by the congregation? What did he do that irritated the staff and congregation the most? What did they like about him? With this information you will have a better idea of your chances of working within this body.
9. Discuss the organizational chart so you are sure about all the accountability factors. If they don't have such a chart, ask the committee to draw one to illustrate the flow of authority. Keep in mind that organizational charts show authority flowing down, and from left to right.
10. How long will you have to decide about your response to the call once the vote has been taken? What percentage will constitute a valid call?
11. Be sure you have the details about the facilities. Where will your office be, who equips it, and what office hours are you expected to keep? Will you have secretarial help and who gets priority on her time?
12. Get any further clarification on the finances that you feel is necessary. What about vacations, travel, further education, entertainment fees, conventions and annual church meetings, days off, sick leave, and housing allowance?

As you seek for this information, it would be wise to keep the following facts in mind. What has been said to the committee and pastor in regard to questioning the candidate also needs to be said to the candidate himself. If you are interested in knowing about the pastor's calling and conducting of staff meetings, don't ask him if he has them. "Yes, sometimes I may." It's far more important to ask what is the regularity of these meetings, and what is the normal agenda? In order to determine the contribution you, the new staff person might have, you might ask in what way the pastor was last influenced by the dialogue in the staff meeting. You want an actual expression of how he was changed by others on the staff. It would also be helpful for you to see a copy of the agenda from the last few meetings.

John came to Calvary Church for four days to be interviewed by the church. He had the opportunity to talk with the congregation. He also had many hours with the search (or calling) committee, who became his major source of information. He made his decision based on what he learned from that committee. The committee members agreed with his desire to see a new progressive ministry. They encouraged him regarding the things he wanted to see done, and gave him much assurance that the congregation would role up their sleeves and work with him. Six months after he came, he began to wonder if the committee had really been honest with him. Few people in the congregation seemed willing to help him implement his plans. The committee had given him the expression of their perspective and interest. They were like most calling committees, a cross-section of the congregation. At least that's what everyone thought. The committee may even have believed that themselves. What John should have understood is that very seldom does the calling committee truly represent the whole congregation. Calling committees are usually made up of a cross-section of the leadership, not of the congregation. They think more aggressively and positively than the average member of the body. They are far more willing to work than most of the congregation.

I've heard many men say after their first year of service in a new church, "If I had only known that, I would never have come to this church." They got their reading from an elite, select section of the congregation.

Because of these facts, it is important to spend time with the people in the congregation. Go to their homes, interview people who don't even ask to see you. Have a hearing with the whole congregation. Remember, you will be working with the members as well as the leaders.

Another caution may prove to be a hard piece of information to get your hands on, but it's worth the effort. Seek to find out who initiated the idea of your position, and why. Even if you will be replacing a vacated position, who was behind the idea of calling another candidate?

If the pastor will be your boss, but the parents are the ones who want a new youth pastor, you can count on the fact that your working relationship is going to be difficult at best. A western church had six youth pastors in three years because each one supposedly couldn't relate to the youth. The church board kept pushing the idea that they needed a youth pastor, but the senior pastor treated each one like dirt because he saw them as an insult to his ministry skills. The board was continually told by the pastor that no worthwhile youth men were available. They were immature, inexperienced lads who didn't know how to minister, according to him. None of those six candidates saw through the situation because they didn't ask the right questions of the right people.

Project for Chapter 12

If your pastor has left, use a questionnaire such as this one to determine your requirements in a candidate.

If you plan to hire a new staff, modify this questionnaire accordingly.

The Congregational Questionnaire

To Members and Friends of First Baptist Church:

What qualities do you consider important in the next pastor of First Baptist?

What direction do you think the total program of the church should take?

The pulpit search committee is eager to know how you feel about these questions. If you will carefully answer the following questions, giving your opinion, it will help us in our effort to find the man who should lead our congregation in the years ahead.

Please number in order of importance (1-8) what you consider to be the most important qualities in a prospective pastor. (Naturally we all consider *all* of them important, but what do you consider *most* important?)

_____ Preaching ability
_____ Worker with young people
_____ Enthusiasm for visitation
_____ Administrative and organizational ability
_____ Personal soul-winner
_____ Willingness and ability to give personal counsel
_____ Warm, friendly personality
_____ Other (please specify)

Would you like First Baptist to have more or less emphasis on the following?

Write "more" for "I would like greater emphasis"
Write "less" for "less emphasis, please"
Write "same" for "about the same as now"

_____ Expository Bible preaching
_____ Evangelistic preaching
_____ Personal evangelism
_____ Group prayer
_____ Social action (involvement with inner city churches, nursing homes, etc.)
_____ Young people's activities
_____ Foreign and home missions
_____ Fellowship activities
_____ Group Bible study
_____ Other (please specify)

Please check the blanks below that describe YOU. (No names, please, unless you desire to be identified.)

_____ Member
_____ Non-member

____ Male
____ Female

Age:
____ Over 50
____ 35 to 50
____ 20 to 35
____ 15 to 20
____ Under 15

If you have an age preference for a pastor, please check:

_____ 25 to 35 ____ 35 to 45 ____ Over 45

Part III: **Maintaining the Team**

13

FINANCIAL EQUITY OF THE TEAM

"Whatever we decide about the pastor's salary, let's keep in mind all those sermons last year on the simple lifestyle."

13

FINANCIAL EQUITY OF THE TEAM

THREE RURAL MINISTERS were having lunch together. They were discussing the common problem of how they were paid. The Methodist minister said, "I draw a line halfway down the aisle. Then I throw all the offering into the air. Everything that comes down on my side, I keep as my pay, and everything that comes down on the other side belongs to God." The Lutheran minister laughed and said, "Isn't that strange, I draw a circle on the platform and I also throw the offering into the air. Everything that lands in the circle is mine and everything else belongs to God." The Baptist burst into laughter and said, "I just throw the offering into the air. Everything that God catches is His and all the rest is mine."

Sometimes I think that would be much easier than trying to determine an equitable way to pay ministers. I was tempted to leave this chapter out of the book, because I knew that no one would agree with me on everything.

I heartily agree with a large church business manager who says that money is emotion. Just touch anyone's finances and you will touch a nerve. Since that's true, it becomes subjective. Consequently it's difficult to come up with firm guidelines that will please both the minister and the congregation. Money is most often mentioned as one of the three major downfalls of a minister. The other two are women and pride. Each one is closely tied to our emotions.

Ever since churches started to pay their pastors, there has been an ongoing argument—the congregation feels the minister is paid too much, and the minister feels he is paid too little. And ever since the era of the multiple staff, that problem has grown more complex and critical, because now is added the problem of equity among the members of the staff.

In the midst of any discussion about what is an equitable salary for their church staff, someone will step forth with a comment such as, "Why can't we just do the Christian thing. After all, aren't these godly people?" The problem is that everyone sees the Christian thing as being different.

The Millers have a yearly income that's less than the pastor. Mr. Miller works sixty hours a week and does an extra good job of managing their finances. They get by comfortably, even though they have one more child than the pastor's family. The Campbells make a little more than the pastor. They have chosen to give a large percentage of their income to charitable causes and live a simple lifestyle. They can't understand why the pastor is pleading for a sizable raise in next year's church budget. No doubt every family in the congregation is comparing its income, expenses, and lifestyle with the pastor's. Because everyone's lifestyle, needs, skills in financial management, values, family size, family background differs, it is just about impossible to get everyone to agree on what is an equitable wage for the church staff.

Also, it is impossible to make a fair value judgment on what constitutes spiritual productivity. Everyone has his own view of what is a fair standard of evaluation. Let's consider these questions: What is the effect of each person's effort in the growth of the church, and what part does the Godhead play in its birth and growth? When that's solved, then maybe we can determine how much each staff member should be paid.

Let's not forget the microcosm model idea either. Isn't the team supposed to model the proper Christian attitude about money, lifestyle, stewardship, and servanthood? Where is the fine line between greed and need? What staff positions are more important than others?

In spite of the complexity of the equity problem, God has given some principles to guide both the hiring church and the working shepherd. These guidelines should be sufficient to help establish godly attitudes and decisions in the church's finances.

Equity of pay for each staff member is determined somewhere between these two tensions—the total giving heart of the sacrificing servant illustrated in Luke 17:7-10, and the "double portion" Timothy was learning about from servant Paul in 1 Timothy 5:17-18.

No member of the clergy is worthy of the title who does not see himself through the eyes of servant in that short parable in Luke. When a servant of God feels he is being paid unfairly, he needs to put himself in the shoes of the servant who prepared the meal for his master when it would seem so much more reasonable for the master to feed the servant, who had worked in the field all day. This is the attitude a servant of God is to have about his work. This definitive parable says a servant should work without any thought of commendation, any feeling of conceit, or wanting any commendation. When he finishes with his day's labor he should say, "I'm not even worthy to be called his servant."

Paul encouraged Timothy as he prepared for the ministry. "The elders who direct the affairs of the church well are worthy of double honor, especially those who work in preaching and teaching"(NIV). That's the other side of the tension. While the staff take their due from Jesus in Luke's Gospel, let the congregation get their dues from Paul. Too often it's just the other way around. No wonder that the staff feel like the muzzled ox (1 Tim. 5:18). They can't "tread out the grain" and thus get the church of Christ built. The first principle for the pastor's salary, then, is anything up to an average wage in your community is not too much.

Back in 1920 in Muncie, Indiana, the pastor's salary was comparable with the superintendent of schools, while today it is comparable with the classroom teacher. The average pastor has higher than average education and higher than average weekly working hours. That ought to make it seem reasonable for a pastor to receive up to the double portion. But again I'm speaking to the church board and congregation, who decide his yearly wage.

Let the pastor, on the other hand, hear the words of 1 Peter 5:2. "Be shepherds of God's flock that is under your care, serving as overseers—not because you are willing, as God wants you to be; not greedy for money, but eager to serve"(NIV). You are not serving a giant corporation. You will never be adequately paid for the work of your labor. Keep your eyes on the mission of the overseer. If you think you are going to be paid for the service, you will only cheapen the meaning of your service.

To keep you from being greedy for money, ask yourself as you bank your salary, "Why am I receiving this paycheck?"

Because I use my spiritual gifts in edifying the church? "But didn't He give them as grace gifts?"

Because I'm productive? "But the spirit of God quickeneth, the flesh profiteth nothing."

Because I built a large congregation? But didn't God build the church?

Because of my faithful long tenure? But "I'm not worthy to be called His servant."

Because I'm more successful or have more stature than another team member? But "let a man not think more highly of himself than he ought."

Because it's equal to what the average pay of the congregation is? But shouldn't we in honor be preferring one another?

In spite of all that, your congregation should honor you by supplying your financial needs so you can give yourself totally to shepherding God's flock. Lyle Schaller has discovered, after polling thousands of congregations, that most of them think too lowly of themselves. Maybe that meager paycheck is a reflection of the church members' own low self-esteem. Maybe they are telling you something about themselves when they are cheap with you, instead of telling you something about yourself.

Because of those two tensions, because it is such a sensitive issue, because it's so hard to get everyone to agree on what equity is, the pastor is wise to keep as low a profile on the team's finances as possible. That's true when you're hiring a new team member and when the yearly budget is presented. You can so seriously hinder your reputation by being too aggressive financially that it can hinder your effectiveness in every kind of evangelistic and nurturing ministry. May you have the spirit of a Methodist pastor who said, "I did real battle with the issue of compensation [hours expected versus pay] nearly twenty years ago, early in my ministry experience, until I realized what it was doing in my inner man. Since then, I've allowed the Lord to fight my battles, and I've learned to be content. My family is far from rich in material goods, but both my family and the church have found me easier to live with."

Determining Equity

It's true that there will never be equity in this world, both in the affairs of the world and in the church, but there are certain guidelines which you can follow to keep peace in your heart, your team, and your congregation. Here are some of them.

1. Be sure to have financial policies established and recorded in your church's policy notebook. They ought to deal with every conceivable financial need.
    a) Do cost of living increases apply to the net or gross salary?
    b) Vacation guidelines. How many weeks to start with and how long before additional time is granted?
    c) When does mandatory retirement come and what retirement benefits can be expected?

- d) When and how is pay increased beyond the cost of living index?
- e) What insurance and social security benefits are paid by the church? How are additional costs on those items cared for?
- f) What conventions and continuing educational costs will be covered by the church?
- g) What special benefits, such as books and entertainment, will the church cover?
- h) If a parsonage is provided, what part of the cost of the upkeep and services can the church be expected to cover?
- i) What auto finances will be covered by the church?

2. The personnel committee should review each team member's finances with him or her each year before the budget is finalized.
3. It is common to base the salary of team members on the local public school salary scale. Keep in mind that the teachers' salaries are based on ten months (nine for teaching and one for vacation), so your scale should be one-sixth more than theirs.
4. The total budget for your team's salary should not be more than 60% of your church's annual budget. In fact, 40% is more ideal.
5. It is common to pay the senior pastor approximately 15% more (total compensation package) than a mature, experienced staff member.
6. Some churches and denominations base their pay scale on other churches of equal size in their area. Be sure you compare the gross compensation package.
7. Keep in mind that professional expenses such as car expense, entertainment, books, and conventions should not be shown on the budget as part of the salary package.
8. If your church is financially unable to pay the yearly expected increase, then it should be added the following year before the financial percentages are figured.
9. It is advisable to put all the salaries in one staff expense figure in the published church budget. Many church people do not understand the complexities of salary packages and thus tend to make poor judgments and comparisons about the staff's compensation. Thus all the salary items of the whole team appear as the one figure in the budget. The details should be on each individual's contract.

10. Since all housing expenses are tax sheltered, this is an additional financial benefit to each pastor. Keep this in mind when you compare salary figures with the average salary of the congregation. That will vary with each family, according to their tax bracket.

Project for Chapter 13

Think through the following information required to complete these work sheets. Then, when budget planning time arrives, you will know what is a fair compensation. You might go over the information with a businessman in your church who is sympathetic to the needs of the ministry.

A Work Sheet to Determine Adequate Support for Our Pastor

Many factors must be considered in determining what support is adequate for a pastor. The provisions should be tailor-made for the community. Care should be exercised when comparing support with other churches, as this may be misleading for several reasons, among them being the difference in average income of the members, and the fact that the other churches may be underpaying their pastors.

Items the Committee Should Note

1. What standard of living must our pastor maintain in order to do his best work in our church?
2. Do we provide enough income to enable him to devote his full time and energy to the church?
3. If he is a young man, he may have to furnish a home, pay off college and seminary debts. Have we thought of this?
4. Are we allowing him enough to provide for his children's future education, to have reserve funds for emergencies, and to make provision for retirement?
5. Remember that the cost of living is continuing to increase about 5% a year. When was the last time we increased his salary?
6. What about additional income? The average pastor receives about $300 per year for weddings and funerals. Would it be better to pay him enough so that he will give these services, especially funerals, without charge to the members?

7. The day of "ministerial discounts" is practically gone—and all for the better. It cheapens the church and embarrasses the pastor to count on such things. Why should the business community subsidize the pastor when the responsibility belongs to the church?
8. Have we taken into account the pastor's training, years of experience, and the size of his family?

I.	BUSINESS COSTS*	
	A. Car expenses	$________
	B. Other travel for the church	$________
	C. Hospitality	$________
	D. Books, magazines, etc.	$________
	E. Pastors, Fellowship membership	$________
	TOTAL	$________
II.	COMPENSATION	
	A. Cash Salary	$________
	B. Housing (Parsonage or cash allowance)	$________
	C. Utilities	$________
	D. Retirement	$________
	E. Insurance (Life and Health)	$________
	F. Other	$________
	TOTAL	$________

*NOTE:
Internal revenue allows 20 cents a mile for the first 15,000 miles and 7 cents beyond that for the business use of a car. The church should allow that much based upon either actual mileage or a prorated monthly estimate. The amount of necessary driving will vary with communities. The car must be insured, kept in good operating condition, tires replaced, and provided with gas and oil. Eventually another car will have to be purchased. If an adequate allowance is not supplied, the pastor will have to pay for the church's services out of his salary.

Other travel, such as district, state, and national meetings in behalf of the church, should be anticipated and fully reimbursed (meals, lodging, and transportation).

Hospitality—When the pastor is expected to do extensive entertaining on behalf of the church, it should provide these costs as business expenses.

Consideration should be given to the amount the pastor spends for books, magazines, etc., for his continual improvement in the ministry. This does not refer to personal enjoyment, but to those items directly related to the ministry.

The total picture based upon minimum expenses for the areas of Professional Expense and Benefits for the pastor is as follows:

Professional Reimbursable Expenses	$4,100
Pastor's Taxable Compensation	$6,645
Benefits For Pastors	$3,000
Minimum Total	$13,745

The areas that are cut more often than not are the Professional Expenses and Benefits for Pastors.

Professional Reimbursable Expenses

Those reimbursed expenses by the church not taxable to the pastor.

1.	Auto expenses: 15,000 miles/yr. = nat'l. average for a pastor at ________/mile to own, operate and maintain a vehicle. (15,000) (.20/mile)	$3,000
2.	Convention expenses will depend upon the motivation of the pastor/staff person, but one convention/yr. is encouraged. This will be a variable figure from year to year, depending upon location and entrance costs. +/− $250-600/yr	$250
3.	Continuing education will depend upon the pastor/staff. This will be a variable figure from year to year. +/− $150 (one week)	$150
4.	Books/Periodicals/Resources will depend upon individual preferences. Five hundred/yr. was the suggested total for a professional staff person.	$500
5.	Discretionary/Hospitality will depend upon the role that the pastor chooses. Estimated minimum cost/mo. is $50. $50 x 12 months	$600
6.	"Other" includes all categories IRS will allow under professional expenses.	$500
		$5,000

Pastor's Taxable Compensation

1.	Cash Salary — taxable area of this section. We will say that $20,000 is the total package of Pastor's compensation.	$15,000

2. Less Housing Costs
   a) Housing allowance/parsonage — this is an inclusive area. It includes home furnishings, lawn mowers, etc., that are used in the parsonage. This should be an exact amount for mortgage, principle and interest, plus the designated amount (which must be spent) for upkeep of the parsonage. Average is $3,600/yr. + taxes. +/– $4800-8400/yr. (4,800)
   b) Utilities allowances include electricity, gas, phone, water, sewage, trash pick-up, etc. Nat'l. average is $1,800/yr. (1,800)
   c) Social Security — offset based upon cash salary x 11.7% (for 1985) (1,755)

Salary less housing cost $6,645

Benefits For Pastors — Non Taxable

1. Retirement Plan Premiums — Some denominational programs are 15% of the Pastor's Salary. On 15,000 this would be 15,000 x .15 = $2,250. Non-taxable annuities should be at least $125.00/mo., if the above plan is not taken—$1,500 $1,500
2. Medical Plan Premiums — are dependent upon the denomination with which one is affiliated. The M & M Board of the ABC is $995/yr. Ministers Life is +/– $600/yr. $600

Minimum total $2,100

The *Leadership* magazine polled their subscribers (Spring of '81) to see what agreement there was between laymen and the clergy about the factors that determine ministerial compensation. Of the 1000 people surveyed, 33% responded. Here were their findings.[1]

Clergy Values	Evaluation Factors	Laity Values
10	Amount of responsibility	10
9	Ability to relate to wide range of problems	9
8	Strength of pulpit ministry	8
7	Ministry results	8
6	Length of service	4
5	Education credentials	5
5	Financial need	6
5	Median income of congregation	5
4	Size of congregation	6
4	Size of budget	7
3	Expertise in specialized ministry	4
2	Size of staff	3
2	Compensation of fellow clergy in denomination	3
1	Age	1

The greatest difference of opinion was in the importance of budget size. This perception reinforces the dichotomy of ministry and money. Pastors think the people don't put enough priority on ministry concerns, the people don't think the pastor puts enough emphasis on numbers (size) and money.

A national trend among American employees shows that employees have become far more aggressive in salary negotiations. All indications show that it is the same with the clergy. If your church has been thoughtful enough to establish a personnel committee, it would be wise for the pastor to discuss with this committee any seeming inequities about his salary package. Some committees or boards are asking each staff person to write a financial position paper. This would show a reflection of each person's current financial situation and his desire or need for any changes.

Major corporations in the seventies found out what servants of God have always known. Money is just a small part of the compensation for service. Dr. Frederick Herzberg stated in an article in the *Harvard Business Review* what six factors must be present to keep people highly motivated: (1) achievement, (2) recognition, (3) the task itself, (4) responsibilitity, (5) advancement, and (6) opportunity for growth.

A congregation and its leadership should readily recognize those factors and continue to encourage their staff in such ways, besides the added financial gains. Congregations that are comprised of a group of management people will quickly pick up on this.

A servant of God who doesn't find those kind of rewards himself no doubt is not very effective in his ministry. Something is wrong with the minister or his ministry when he has to beg for that recognition. When peoples' hearts are responding to God's Word and they are becoming disciples of Christ through the ministry events of the team, there should be sufficient compensation for the team. A true microcosm team will provide plenty of encouragement to its fellow laborers in their weekly routine. Team members will need to learn to rejoice with those who rejoice and weep with those who weep. What better way can they show true body life!

It is a common game, and known among a large percentage of the laity, that the best way to get rid of a pastor who has more than served his time is to withhold his annual raises. It has become even more common in recent years to simply ask the incompetent minister to leave. Unfortunately, there doesn't seem to be a pleasant way to do that, but it must be done according to the church's constitution. That should call for a congregational vote where there is congregational rule. The minister should be visited by the official church board or the personnel committee. They have a serious obligation to show just cause when they ask him to leave. Even though the vote of the congregation is not a majority, but sizable representation of the body, the staff person is wise to leave in a peaceful manner. He may feel he is in a proper position to stay and is not inadequate for the task, yet if he chooses to fight for his rights, he will only damage the cause of Christ, both in the church and the community. Thousands of individuals and their whole families have given up their church attendance and often their faith in Christ, because a minister chose to prove he was right. He may win the battle but lose the war. In the true spirit of Christ he will quietly pack his belongings without a vindictive spirit and trust that vengence still belongs to the Lord and that He will repay. Here is an acid test which will show whether the man of God has come to serve or to have his own needs and rights served. The only exception to this rule is when an obvious doctrinal issue is at stake. However, church historians say that a large majority of church fights and splits are over personality conflicts, and that calling it a point of doctrine is only a cover-up for an unrelated issue.

Special Considerations

As our nation's cultural and economic conditions change, the pastor faces new and varied situations with his financial affairs. By the time this book is published, he may need to look at some additional major changes.

Since 1979, most economic consultants believe that young families in America will have a difficult time purchasing their own homes. The trend away from churches owning parsonages may soon be back with us. *Leadership's* survey, mentioned earlier in this chapter, discovered that 62% of the pastors who answered that survey are living in parsonages. Because of many creative ways to finance homes in this decade, churches can aid their staffs in owning their own living quarters.

Some churches have provided down payments to staff members, with the agreement that when the house is sold, the church will receive that money back with its accumulated appreciation or interest. Sometimes that money has come from the sale of the old parsonage, or a member of the congregation has loaned the money, with varied conditions attached.

Another cultural shift that has recently occurred has been the increase in the women's work force. Two-income families have become a way of life in America. Although the *Leadership* magazine survey found that 96% of the laymen thought it would be best if the pastor's wife not work outside the home, nearly 50% of pastors' wives have their own vocation. An interesting point is that they state they are doing so for their own personal growth and achievement, rather than because they need additional finances. It has generally seemed more acceptable for an associate's wife to work. Since the laity still feel that the pastor's wife belongs in the manse, discuss this matter with the church before accepting a call. Otherwise, it could cause hard feelings later on.

In a large church in a Western state, the pastor's wife is employed as an executive secretary in a large firm, yet she still finds time to direct the musical program in the church. That seems to make the congregation feel better about her employment. Tension develops when a pastor's working wife is seldom involved in the life and ministry of the church.

Sabbatical leaves have long been popular for professors, but it is only in recent years that it is becoming popular for pastors. So far, a sabbatical is generally for a pastor with long tenure, in a large church, who's interested in doing advanced study. It is not uncommon for all staff members to be granted time and expenses for a course or two at a local institution, or for attending a seminar of their choosing some place in the country. Some choose to do that rather than going to their denominational yearly gathering, while others are afforded the opportunity of attending both. With the increased popularity of the Theology of Ministries degree, we should expect to see an increase in study leaves.

More churches are facing the fact that their staff may have extended illnesses, and consequently exorbitant cost. Therefore many have taken precautions in the pastor's contract to deal with such an eventuality. That can prove a sticky situation if guidelines are not established before the illness occurs. Of course, the closer to the beginning of his charge the more difficult an extended disability is to deal with. A real struggle can result between what is equitable and what the budget can really handle. This all points to the urgency for the church to make necessary insurance arrangements when a person joins the staff.

Harvey has served his church for over twenty years and has now reached retirement age. All these years he has been cared for in a good parsonage. He has had small increases in salary, but the church was never able to help him invest in any retirement program other than social security. The church was caught in a changing neighborhood and has not prospered. He cannot afford to retire, even though he needs to do so, both for his own well-being and because the church needs new and younger leadership. It would help now if Harvey had been able to start his own retirement. Far too many churches and staff persons will face retirement difficulties in their later years unless precautions are taken early in their ministries.

Personal Finances

Whether you like it or not, when you take any pastoral position, your whole life becomes a model to your congregation. Being a model steward of your finances is one of the most difficult areas to deal with. When Paul admonished Timothy to live his life above reproach, part of that charge had to do with his relationship to money. The encouragement to be temperate probably also included the wise use of his finances. Then Paul suggested that he not be a lover of money. Timothy was to have a good reputation with his neighbors, as well. (See 1 Timothy 3:2-7.) How can you do that if you don't share what God has given you, and you don't pay your bills? It seems as if a community will forgive a minister for many things, but never for not paying his bills.

It would be most advisable, then, for a servant of God to establish a budget and learn to live within the confines of that budget. Far too many men ask for more money when families in the congregation with far less means get by much better. These pastors have not learned to manage their finances. A team that develops a close caring community among themselves ought to provide council, admonition, and encouragement in financial matters, just as much as they do in spiritual matters. Someone in the congregation may be a financier who could provide the consultation necessary to help you become wise in managing your money. You will not only help yourself, but pay him a great compliment by calling on him for help. Many people have not yet learned that it isn't how much money you have, but how well you manage what you do have, that makes it possible to live a comfortable life.

Another way you need to be a model to your church family is in your giving. It's upsetting to hear a minister say that, since he gives his whole life to the Lord as a servant, he needn't practice tithing. You can't teach the congregation to practice stewardship if you don't do so yourself. The congregation may not know what you give, but it's amazing how they find out if you don't give. If you live in a parsonage, that's part of your income. Do you give to God a percent of that income also? The Lord never sets the line, He leaves that to us. Don't ask the congregation to stretch their faith, unless you trust the Lord to do the same with you.

For a team to function as a team, rules are needed. One of the major rules should deal with the way you handle charges for extra services. It will soon be known if one team member accepts fees for funerals and weddings, while another doesn't. If the congregation pays you well, it would seem wise to render certain services free to families who are church members.

Charles was a gracious and well-beloved pastor who served the Elm Street Church for many years before he retired. His parents had died mid-way through the years of his ministry there. They left him with an inheritance which enabled him to be financially independent. He chose to accept only a meager salary during his remaining years. He would have done the church a favor by receiving the normal salary with its usual increases, and then giving the money to mission endeavors. When Charles retired, the congregation had lost the art and joy of giving, and now they were not able to provide a living wage to a new pastor.

The church almost died because it could not afford a capable shepherd to lead the flock.

It is rare for a staff member to move to another parish without receiving a raise in pay. When a person has neared the end of his career and takes a smaller responsibility, or when a person sees a promising challenge, he may choose to accept a lesser wage. Unfortunately, ministers in general have a poor reputation at this point. Too many show that they do indeed love money, because they leave a good solid ministry for a church which entices them away by offering a larger salary package. A minister may undo all his years of teaching on godly values by one greedy decision to move to another charge so he can have a bigger income and a better lifestyle, and then charge it off to God. "Well, I would never have moved if I didn't feel it was His will." A true man of God will show great concern in all of his financial affairs, so that God will be honored in his life and ministry.

Appendix

PHILOSOPHY OF MINISTRY*

Six Cardinal Principles

Introduction—

Why Do We Need a Philosophy of Ministry?

A. In order to understand all that God has to say about various subjects (the Second Coming, sin, etc.) it is necessary to study the Bible topically. This type of study is often called Systematic Theology. In this case, we are attempting to study all that the Bible has to say about ministry. We could call this our Theology or Philosophy ("the general principles of a field of knowledge"—Webster's) of Ministry.

B. Unfortunately, ministry is an area that many Christians have not studied topically or systematically. As a result, their Philosophy of Ministry is poorly developed and not well grounded on the Scriptures. It is often nothing more than programs and structures, with little understanding of underlying biblical principles.

C. Finally, these six cardinal principles are not the final word. They represent a beginning statement of our Philosophy of Ministry. It is likely that they will be modified and expanded as time goes on.

I. The Starting Point of Our Ministry is God—Not Human Activity (1 Cor. 3:6)

A. *God's Part*: God's goals for the Christian are superhuman (1 Peter 2:21; 1 John 3:16; Eph. 5:18-20). As a matter of fact, Christian growth is totally beyond the realm of

---

*This "Philosophy of Ministry" of the South Evangelical Presbyterian Fellowship, Englewood, Co., is used with permission and is "continually undergoing evaluation and improvement," according to the Senior Pastor of the church, Dr. Dale D. Scheafer.

human effort (Gal. 3:1-5) for apart from Christ we can do nothing (John 15:5). Ministry and spiritual growth are things that God does by means of the Holy Spirit (1 Thess. 1:5; Titus 3:5).

B. *Man's Part*: God, in graciousness, has allowed man to have a part in the work and ministry of His Kingdom (2 Cor. 5:20). Our part is to abide in Christ (John 15:5) and to rely on the Spirit to bring change (Gal. 5:18, 22-23). We abide in Christ as we abide in the Word of God (1 John 2:24) and as we obey that which Christ tells us to do (1 John 3:24; John 15:10).

C. *Implications for Ministry*

1. Realize that you are unqualified to minister to anyone (2 Cor. 3:5-6) and that only God can bring growth in another's life (1 Cor. 3:6).
2. Recognize that God's grace equips us for ministry (Rom. 1:5; 12:6) and that we can do all things in Christ who strengthens us (Phil. 4:13).
3. Determine to abide in Christ (John 15:4-5) by living in moment-by-moment dependence on God (Prov. 3:5-6). Commit yourself to the Word and prayer (Acts 6:4).
4. Remember that without God, I cannot. Without me, God will not.

II. The Guide For Our Ministry Is the Bible—Not Human Wisdom (Isa. 55:6-11)

A. *The inspiration of the Bible*: Because the Bible is inspired by God (God breathed) (2 Tim. 3:16-17), it is the final authority for Christian *faith* and *practice.* It must be interpreted correctly (2 Peter 3:16) with the help of the Holy Spirit (1 Cor. 2:12-13; Eph. 1:18).

B. *The Bible as God's "message book"*: Since the Bible is the final authority for Christian *faith*, it serves as the ultimate judge as to what we believe as truth (John 16:13; 2 Peter 1:20-21); therefore, all experiences and circumstances must be interpreted in the light of what the Scriptures state (1 Cor. 14:29; Deut. 13:1-3). By saying that the Bible is God's "message book," we are saying that it gives us the content or the "what" of the Christian life (what is the nature of God, the nature of man, etc.).

C. *The Bible as God's "method book"*: Since the Bible is the final authority for Christian *practice*, it serves as the ultimate judge as to what principles direct our methods of ministry (2 Cor. 1:12). By saying that the Bible is God's "method book," we are saying that it gives us the process of the "how" of the Christian life.

In talking about methods, we must also distinguish between absolutes and non-absolutes. *Absolutes* are the foundational biblical principles that do not vary with time or culture. "Christians should gather together" (Heb. 10:24-25). *Non-absolutes* are the specific applications which may vary with time or culture. "Christians should gather together at 11:00 A.M. on Sunday morning and sit in pews." The absolutes are eternal and unchanging. On the other hand, we should have great freedom to change the non-absolutes, depending on the need of a particular situation.

III. The Focus of Our Ministry Is People—Not Programs (1 Thess. 2:8; John 3:16)

"At the heart of the universe is a Person, not natural forces, a Creator who reveals Himself to persons, who became a human Person in Christ, who seeks to redeem estranged, sinful persons back to Himself. . . Essentially, the church is not a building, nor an institution, an organization, a program. Essentially the church is people . . . it is natural to describe the local church in terms of its activities, its work, as an institution; but, everything the church does is for the sake of people. All programming and organization are means to the end of effecting changes in people. The focus must always be on people."

(LeBar, *Focus on People in Church Education*, p.11)

IV. The Goal of Our Ministry Is Mature Christians—Not Simply Converts (Col. 1:28-29)

The Westminster Confession states that man's chief end is to glorify God and to enjoy Him forever. We glorify God by developing people, both ourselves and others, who are becoming more like Christ (John 15:8). In Matthew 28:19-20, this is called making disciples. One way of describing a "disciple" is that he is a person who lives life according to biblical priorities. These priorities fall into four categories:

1. Progressive commitment to Jesus Christ (Matt. 6:33; Luke 9:23)
2. Progressive commitment to the family (1 Tim. 5:8; Deut. 6:23)

3. Progressive commitment to the Body of Christ (Gal. 6:10)
4. Progressive commitment to the work of Christ in the world (Acts 1:8)

Further comments on the fourth priority: To be committed to the *work of Christ in the world* means to be committed to *both* social concern and evangelism. Both of these grow out of community.

"Community is the matrix of mission. A congregation without community cannot fulfill its evangelistic mission, whatever is done to exhort or train. Conversely, when a congregation is spiritually healthy, that is, committed to Jesus Christ and to each other and constrained by love to selfless concern for all mankind, evangelism will happen spontaneously, effortlessly, continuously, and effectively. Not only will the life of the community attract the alienated and lonely to its accepting, reconciling warmth, but in dispersion its members will radiate that redemptive love infectiously to the world."

V. The Environment for Our Ministry Is the Corporate Body—Not Individualism (Rom. 12:3-8)

A. *We must be the people of God before we do the work of God.* Too often we move into ministry before we have taken time to be the community of God. Jesus said that the world would know that we are His disciples if we love one another (John 13:34-35). He repeats this concept in John 17:21 when He says that the world will know that He was sent by the Father when they see the unity of the believers. This principle was then illustrated in the early church (Acts 2:24-27).

B. *Every member is a minister.* The ministry is not just for the seminary-trained professional. God has gifted *every* Christian (Rom. 12:3-8; 1 Cor. 12:7-11) so that each might have a part in building up the Body of Christ. Everyone is essential and unique in this process.

C. *God has called some to leadership.* In the Bible, the leader is first of all a servant. He is committed to making others successful. He serves by pastoring the flock (1 Peter 5:2-4), and by equipping the saints for their ministries (Eph. 4:11-12). A leader must measure up to certain qualifications (1 Tim. 3:1-7; Titus 1:5-9). It seems clear that the biblical norm is for a multiplicity of leadership (1 Tim. 5:17) and that decisions ideally should be made by the unanimous consent of those in leadership (Acts 15:23-25). This requires teamwork and implies that the leadership should be committed to the same basic body of doctrine and philosophy of ministry (Amos 3:3).

D. *Authority and Submission*: Because God has given leaders to oversee the flock, those under their authority should submit to their leadership (Heb. 13:17; 1 Peter 5:5; Rom. 13:1-7). The only exception to this is when the leadership is calling the people to do something which would result in their clear disobedience of a biblical absolute.

VI. The Process of Our Ministry Is Spiritual Reproduction—Not Spiritual Addition (2 Tim. 2:2)

A. *Definitions*

1. *A Convert*: One who has realized that because he was a sinner, he was subject to the wrath of God. Seeing his desperate plight and his inability to save himself, he placed his trust in the finished work of Christ.
2. *A Mature Christian*: One who realizes that he still lives in his sinful nature and that he cannot live the Christian life in his own strength. Realizing his desperate plight, he places his trust moment by moment in the finished work of Christ. He has also developed the necessary disciplines of the Christian life so that the lifelong process of maturing in Christlikeness can reasonably be expected to continue. He has become independently dependent on Christ.
3. *Spiritual Addition*: The process of reproducing in others what the Spirit of God is doing in you so that they have become either converts or mature Christians. This is also known as second generation discipleship.
4. *Spiritual Reproduction*: The process of reproducing in others what the Spirit of God is doing in you and in turn enabling them to reproduce it in a third generation. This is also known as third generation discipleship.

B. *Why emphasize spiritual reproduction?*

Let us suppose it takes two years to help a person grow spiritually to the place where he can reproduce also. Then if you invest your life in another:	Let us suppose you can lead one person to Christ each day, but by doing this, you don't have time to help him or her grow. Then:
After 2 years there will be 2 mature Christians;	there will be 731 converts
After 4 years there will be 4 mature Christians;	there will be 1,462 converts
After 10 years there will be 32 mature Christians;	there will be 3,653 converts
After 20 years there will be 1,024 mature Christians;	there will be 7,306 converts
After 30 years there will be 32,768 mature Christians.	there will be 10,958 converts

C. *How to emphasize spiritual reproduction*

1. By developing the personal vision to be involved in third generation discipleship. This comes from realizing the long range impact of spiritual multiplication.
2. By learning to think relationally. "As one begins to think relationally rather than terminally, he will become more and more aware of the fantastic power and life-changing potential which can be realized by the application of this truth. He will see how an individual who learns to think relationally can reach extremely high levels of commitment and accomplish tremendous feats of achievement. Secular men have taken this truth, which was intended to be used by the believer, and used it to make money or to gain a position of power."

   (Hartman & Sutherland, *A Guidebook to Discipleship*, p. 34)
3. By being willing to pay the cost of investing your life in individuals (Luke 10:30; 1 Thess. 2:1-12). ". . . there are certain demands that cannot be overlooked in

such a ministry (of multiplication). Perhaps the most important is the requirement that you spend much time with one person to build him. You are making a conscious choice to restrict your other ministries and stake your future productivity on the faithful ministries of those whom you build. . . To make the wrong selection is to submit yourself to a fruitless and unrewarding ministry."

(Kuhne, *The Dynamics of Discipleship Training*, p. 21)

NOTES

Chapter 1

1. Dody Donnelly, C.S.J. *Team: Theory and Practice of Team Ministry* (New York: Paulist Press, 1977, pp. 52-53.

Chapter 3

1. Reprinted from *Team: Theory and Practice of Team Ministry*, by Dody Donnelly, C.S.J., ©.1977 by the Missionary Society of St. Paul the Apostle in the State of New York. Used by permission of Paulist Press.
2. Richards, Lawrence. *Youth Ministry: Its Renewal in the Local Church* (Grand Rapids: Zondervan, 1972) pp. 125-127.
3. *Ibid.*, p.
4. *Ibid.*, p.

Chapter 5

1. Charles Loomis, *Modern Social Theories* (Princeton: Van Nostrand, 1961), pp. 3ff.
2. Alan Lay McGinnis, *Friendship Factor* (Minneapolis: Augsburg Publishing House, 1979).
3. Larry Richards, *Youth Ministry* (Grand Rapids: Zondervan, 1972), p. 34.
4. Reprinted from *Team: Theory and Practice of Team Ministry*, pp. 52-53, by Dody Donnelly, C.S.J., ©. by The Missionary Society of St. Paul the Apostle in the State of New York. Used by permission.
5. Darwin Cartwright and Alvin Zander, *Group Dynamics: Research and Theory* (Evanston: Row, Peterson and Co., 1960), pp. 402-410.

Chapter 10

1. Howard Hendricks, *Leadership* (Summer, 1980), pp. 100ff.
2. Gilbert Martin, *Leadership* (Spring, 1981), pp. 82ff.

Chapter 11

1. Herman Street, *The Multiple Staff in the Local Church* (Philadelphia: Westminster Press, 1963), pp. 67-68.
2. *Ibid.*

Chapter 13

1. *Leadership* Journal, Vol. 2, number 2, p. 42. Used with permission.

BIBLIOGRAPHY

Blanchard, Kenneth, Ph.D. and Johnson, Spencer, M.D. *The One Minute Manager*. New York: Berkley Books, 1981.

Butt, Howard. *The Velvet Covered Brick*. New York: Harper & Row, 1973.

Brown, Jerry W. *Church Staff Teams That Win*. Nashville: Convention Press, 1979.

Carroll, Jackson W. and Wilson, Robert L. *Too Many Pastors*? New York: The Pilgrim Press, 1980.

Cartwright, Dorwin and Zander, Alvin. *Group Dynamics: Research and Theory*. Evanston: Row, Peterson and Company, 1960.

Donnelly, C.S.J., Dody. *Team: Theory and Practice of Team Ministry*. New York: Paulist Press, 1977.

Getz, Gene A. *Building Up One Another*. Wheaton: Ill. Victor Books, 1973.

Griffin, Em. *Getting Together; A Guide for Good Groups*. Downers Grove, Ill. Inter-Varsity Press, 1982.

Hersey, Paul and Blanchard, Kenneth H. *Management of Organizational Behavior: Utilizing Human Resources*. New Jersey: Prentice-Hall, Inc., Fourth Edition, 1982.

Judy, Murlene O. *The Multiple Staff Ministry*. New York: Abingdon Press, 1969.

Loomis, Charles. *Modern Social Theories*. Princeton: VanNostrand, 1961.

McGinnis, Alan Ray. *Friendship Factor*. Minneapolis: Augsburg Publishing House, 1979

Miller, Arthur F. and Mattson Ralph T. *The Truth About You*. Old Tappan, New Jersey: Fleming H. Revell Company, 1972.

Milton, Mayeroff. *On Caring*. New York: Perennial Library, 1971.

Peters, Thomas J. and Waterman, Robert H. Jr. *In Search of Excellence*. New York: Harper & Row, 1982.

Richards, Larry. *Youth Ministry*. Grand Rapids: Zondervan Publishing House, 1972.

Rush, Myron. *Management: A Biblical Approach*.

Schaller, Lyle E. *Survival Tactics in the Parish*. Nashville: Abingdon, 1977.

_______________. *The Multiple Staff and the Larger Church*. Nashville: Abingdon, 1980.

Shtogren, John A. *Models for Management; The Structure of Competence*. Texas: Teleometrics Int'l., 1980.

Sweet, Herman J. *The Multiple Staff in the Local Church*. Philadelphia: The Westminister Press, 1963.

Wakefield, Norman. *Listening; A Christian's Guide to Loving Relationships*. Waco: Word, 1981.

Wedel, Leonard E. *Church Staff Administration; Practical Approaches*. Nashville: Broadman Press, 1978